T0016439

EYEWITNESS
HUMAN
BODY

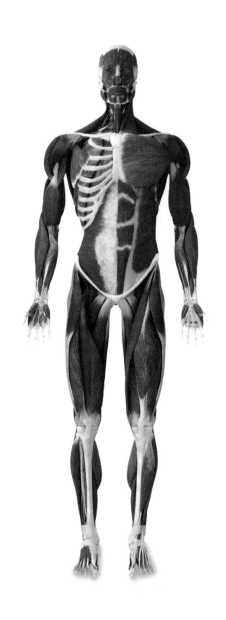

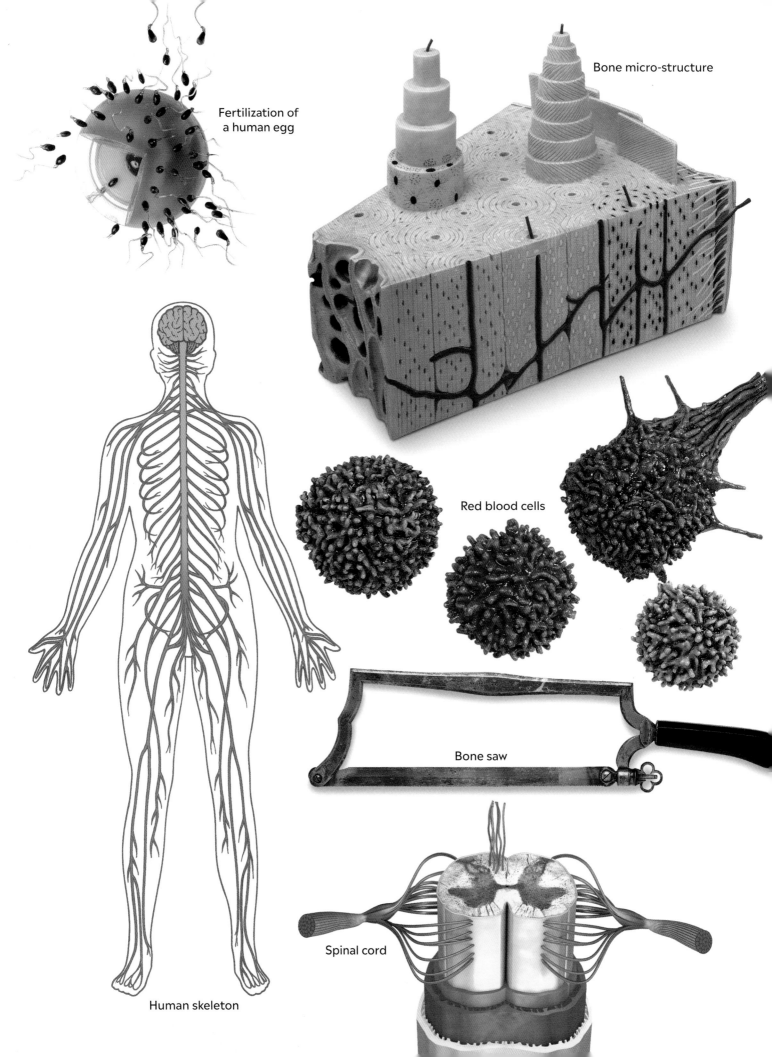

Fertilization of a human egg

Bone micro-structure

Red blood cells

Bone saw

Human skeleton

Spinal cord

EYEWITNESS

HUMAN
BODY

Written by
Richard Walker

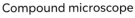
Compound microscope

Nerve cell

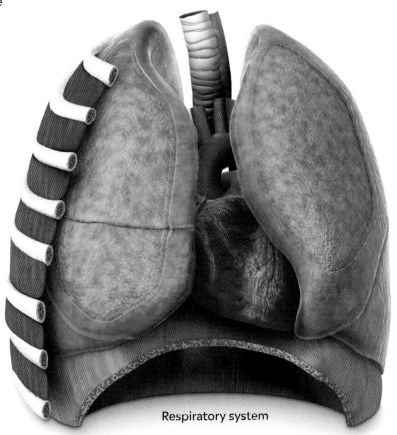
Respiratory system

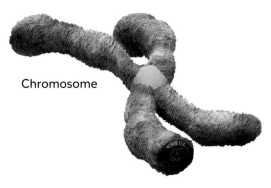

Chromosome

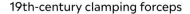

19th-century clamping forceps

REVISED EDITION

DK DELHI

Senior Editor Sreshtha Bhattacharya
Senior Art Editor Vikas Chauhan
Project Art Editor Heena Sharma
Editor Bipasha Roy
Picture Researcher Vishal Ghavri
Managing Editor Kingshuk Ghoshal
Managing Art Editor Govind Mittal
DTP Designers Ashok Kumar, Pawan Kumar, Rakesh Kumar
Jackets Designer Deepak Mittal
Senior Jackets Coordinator Priyanka Sharma-Saddi

DK LONDON

Senior Editor Carron Brown
Editor Kelsie Besaw
Art Editor Chrissy Checketts
US Editor Heather Wilcox
US Executive Editor Lori Cates Hand
Managing Editor Francesca Baines
Managing Art Editor Philip Letsu
Senior Production Editor Andy Hilliard
Senior Production Controller Poppy David
Senior Jackets Designer Surabhi Wadhwa-Gandhi
Jacket Design Development Manager Sophia MTT
Publisher Andrew Macintyre
Associate Publishing Director Liz Wheeler
Art Director Karen Self
Publishing Director Jonathan Metcalf

Consultant Dr. Kristina Routh
Authenticity Reader Kit Heyam

FIRST EDITION

Editor Lisa Stock
Project Editor Jane Yorke
Art Editor David Ball
Senior Editor Rob Houston
Senior Art Editor Alison Gardner
Managing Editor Camilla Hallinan
Managing Art Editor Owen Peyton Jones
Art Director Martin Wilson
Category Publisher Andrew Macintyre
Picture Researcher Louise Thomas
Production Editor Hitesh Patel
Senior Production Controller Pip Tinsley
Jacket Designer Andy Smith
Jacket Editor Adam Powley

This Eyewitness Book® has been conceived by
Dorling Kindersley Limited and Editions Gallimard

This American Edition, 2023
First American Edition, 2009
Published in the United States by DK Publishing
1745 Broadway, 20th Floor, New York, NY 10019

Copyright © 2009, 2014, 2023 Dorling Kindersley Limited
DK, A Division of Penguin Random House LLC
23 24 25 26 27 10 9 8 7 6 5 4 3 2 1
001-335447–Apr/2023

Some of the material in this book previously appeared in
Eyewitness Human Body, published in 1993, 2004.

All rights reserved.
Without limiting the rights under the copyright reserved above,
no part of this publication may be reproduced, stored in
or introduced into a retrieval system, or transmitted,
in any form, or by any means (electronic, mechanical,
photocopying, recording, or otherwise), without the
prior written permission of the copyright owner.
Published in Great Britain by Dorling Kindersley Limited.

A catalog record for this book is available from the Library of Congress.
ISBN 978-0-7440-7991-3 (Paperback)
ISBN 978-0-7440-7992-0 (ALB)

DK books are available at special discounts when purchased in
bulk for sales promotions, premiums, fund-raising, or educational
use. For details, contact: DK Publishing Special Markets,
1745 Broadway, 20th Floor, New York, NY 10019
SpecialSales@dk.com

Printed and bound in China

For the curious
www.dk.com

MIX
Paper | Supporting
responsible forestry
FSC™ C018179

This book was made with Forest
Stewardship Council™ certified
paper—one small step in DK's
commitment to a sustainable future.
For more information, go to
www.dk.com/our-green-pledge.

Cross-section of the skin

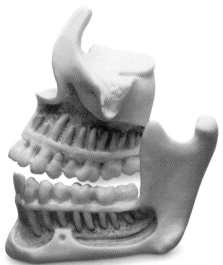

Adult teeth

Balanced diet

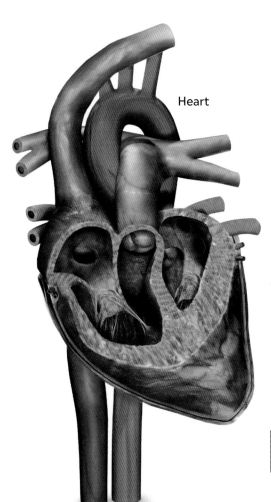

Heart

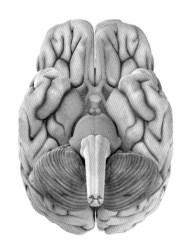

Brain from below

Contents

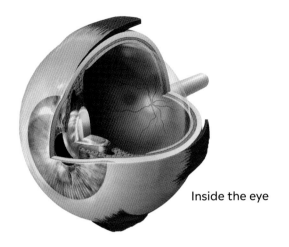

Inside the eye

The human body

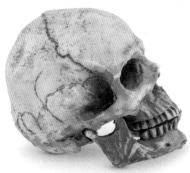

Human origins

Human beings are all related. We belong to the species *Homo sapiens* and are descendants of the first modern humans, who lived in Africa 300,000 years ago and migrated across the globe.

We may look different from the outside, but our bodies are all constructed in the same way. The study of anatomy, which explores body structure, shows that internally, we are virtually identical—apart from differences in reproductive organs. The study of physiology reveals how body systems combine to keep our cells, and us, alive.

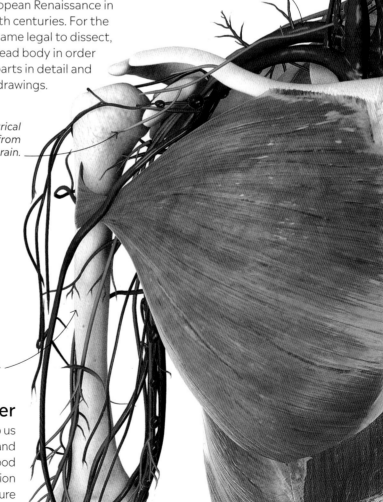

Eye is a light-detecting sense organ.

Vein carries the blood toward the heart.

Artery carries the blood away from the heart.

Understanding anatomy

The modern study of anatomy dates back to the European Renaissance in the 15th and 16th centuries. For the first time, it became legal to dissect, or cut open, a dead body in order to examine its parts in detail and make accurate drawings.

Muscular system   Skeletal system

Nerve carries electrical signals to and from the brain.

The body as a building

In 1708, physiologists likened the body to a household—bringing in supplies (eating food), distributing essentials (the blood system), creating warmth (body chemical processes), and organizing everyone (the brain).

Bone supports the upper arm.
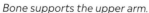
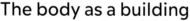

Working together

Our internal organs and systems work together to keep us alive. Bones, muscles, and cartilage provide support and movement. Nerves carry control signals. The heart and blood vessels deliver food and oxygen. The result of this cooperation is a balanced internal environment, with a constant temperature of about 98.6°F (37°C). This enables cells to work at their best.

Body make-up

It takes around 100 trillion cells to build a human body. There are 200 different types of these microscopic living units, each of which is highly complex. Similar cells join together to make a tissue, two or more tissues form an organ, and linked organs create a system. The body has 12 systems.

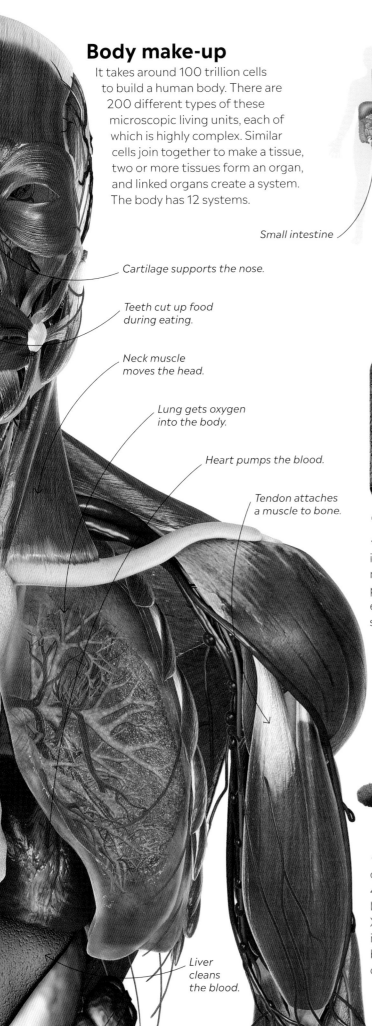

Cartilage supports the nose.

Teeth cut up food during eating.

Neck muscle moves the head.

Lung gets oxygen into the body.

Heart pumps the blood.

Tendon attaches a muscle to bone.

Liver cleans the blood.

1 System

Along with the digestive system, the other 11 are the skin, skeletal, muscular, nervous, hormonal, circulatory, lymphatic, immune, respiratory, urinary, and reproductive systems. The role of the digestive system is to break down food so it can be used by body cells.

Small intestine

2 Organ

The small intestine is a long digestive tube. It completes the breakdown of food into simple substances, which are absorbed into the blood. Muscle tissue in the wall of the small intestine pushes food along it.

3 Tissue

The lining of the small intestine has millions of microscopic fingerlike projections called villi. This epithelial tissue provides a vast surface for absorbing food.

4 Cells

The epithelial cells that cover a villus sit tightly together, which stops food and digestive juices from leaking through to the tissues that support these cells.

5 Chromosome

The control centre, or nucleus, of every cell has 46 chromosomes. These long threads (coiled up in an X-shape above) contain coded instructions, called genes, for building our cells, tissues, organs, and systems.

6 DNA

Each chromosome consists of deoxyribonucleic acid (DNA), a molecule. DNA's strands are linked by chemicals called bases (shown here in yellow, green, blue, and red). Their sequence provides a gene's coded instructions.

Early healers

This cave painting from Brandberg Mountain in Namibia is more than 2,000 years old. It is thought to show an African shaman or medicine man.

Myth, magic, and medicine

Early humans made sculptures and cave paintings of human figures. As civilizations grew, people began to study their own bodies closely, but care for the sick and injured was tied up with myths, superstition, and a belief that gods or demons sent illnesses. Ancient Greek physician Hippocrates (c. 460–c. 375 BCE) taught that diseases could be identified and treated. In the Roman world, Galen (129–c. 216 CE) set out ideas about anatomy and physiology that would last for centuries. In Persia, medical knowledge was developed by such physicians as Ibn Sina (980–1037 CE).

Holes in the head

This 4,000-year-old skull from Jericho, West Bank, shows the results of trepanning, or drilling holes in the skull. Modern surgery uses a similar technique, called craniotomy, to release pressure in the brain caused by bleeding.

Sacred sacrifice

In the 14th and 15th centuries, the Aztecs of Mexico believed the god Huitzilopochtli would make the sun rise and bring them victory, if they offered him human and animal sacrifices. The Aztecs might have learned about the inner organs of the body from these rituals.

The brain, regarded as useless, was hooked out through the nostrils and discarded.

The heart, considered the center of being, was left inside the chest.

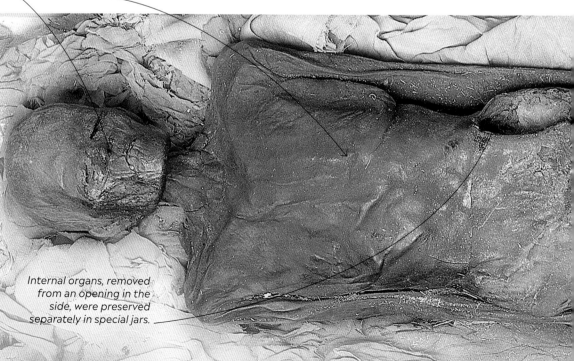

Egyptian embalming

Some 5,000 years ago, the Egyptians believed that a dead body remained home to its owner's soul in the afterlife, but only if preserved as a lifelike mummy. Natron, a type of salt, was used to dry out the body to embalm it and stop it from rotting.

Internal organs, removed from an opening in the side, were preserved separately in special jars.

Chinese channels

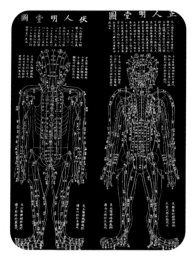

Written more than 2,300 years ago, *The Yellow Emperor's Classic of Internal Medicine* explains acupuncture treatments, which focus on the flow of chi, or vital energy, along 12 body channels, or meridians. Needles are inserted into the skin along these meridians to rebalance the body forces known as Yin (cool and female) and Yang (hot and male).

 EYEWITNESS

Claudius Galen

Born in ancient Greece, Claudius Galen became a towering figure in the study of anatomy, physiology, and medicine in Rome. There, he treated gladiators as a young physician, describing their wounds as "windows into the body." Human dissection was banned, so he studied the anatomy of animals instead. His flawed ideas were accepted without question across Europe for 1,500 years.

Translated into Latin in the 12th century, *The Canon of Medicine* was the leading medical textbook for the next five centuries.

Medieval treatments

Blood-letting, using a knife or a blood-sucking worm called a leech, was a traditional, if brutal, remedy for all manner of ills in medieval times. Few physicians tried to see if the treatment was of any benefit to the patient.

An illustrated panel invokes God for the completion of the work.

A medical textbook

This is a page from an 18th-century copy of the *Al-Qanun fi al-Tibb* (*The Canon of Medicine*), written by the Persian physician Ibn Sina in c.1025. He built on the knowledge of ancient physicians, such as Galen and Hippocrates. The massive book consisted of five volumes covering different topics on health and sickness and the human body's anatomy and function.

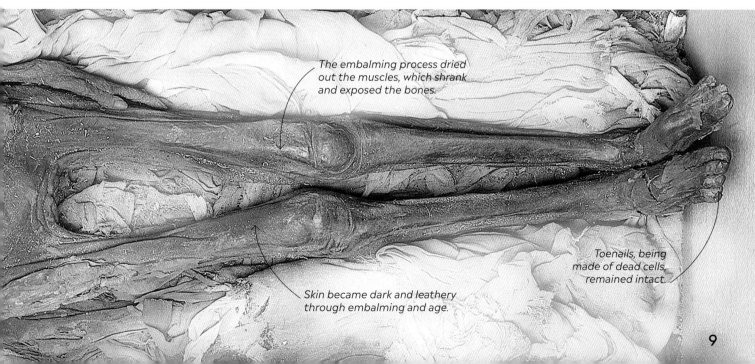

The embalming process dried out the muscles, which shrank and exposed the bones.

Toenails, being made of dead cells, remained intact.

Skin became dark and leathery through embalming and age.

Respect for death

For many in the Middle Ages, life was less important than death and ascent into heaven. The body housed the soul and must not be dissected. This anatomist risked being punished.

Study and dissection

A rebirth of the arts and science, which had been flourishing in Asia, spread across Europe between the 14th and 17th centuries. The ban on human dissection (cutting open a body to study its structure) was relaxed. In Italy, Andreas Vesalius (1514–1564) performed dissections and drew conclusions based on his observations. By correcting centuries-old accepted views, he revolutionized the science of anatomy and began a new era in medicine.

Anatomical theater

Mondino dei Liuzzi (c. 1270–1326), a professor at Bologna, Italy, introduced the public dissection of human corpses and is known as the Restorer of Anatomy. By the late 16th century, anatomical theaters were built at many universities. This 1610 engraving shows an anatomical theater in which the spectators are looking down at a dissection in progress.

Tools of the trade

These 19th-century surgical instruments each have their own role, from cutting through bones to probing tiny nerves and blood vessels. Today's surgeons use a similar but broader range of instruments, making use of modern technology, such as power saws and laser scalpels.

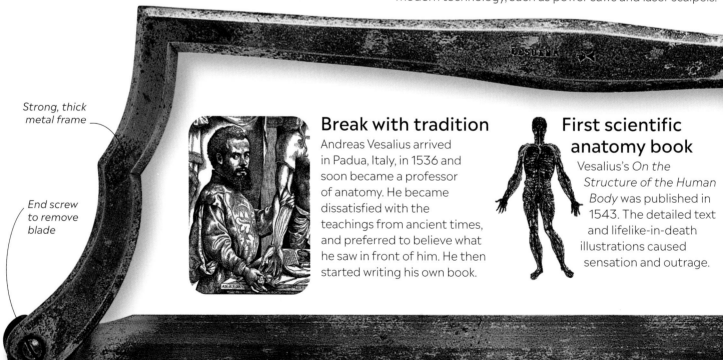

Strong, thick metal frame

End screw to remove blade

Break with tradition

Andreas Vesalius arrived in Padua, Italy, in 1536 and soon became a professor of anatomy. He became dissatisfied with the teachings from ancient times, and preferred to believe what he saw in front of him. He then started writing his own book.

First scientific anatomy book

Vesalius's *On the Structure of the Human Body* was published in 1543. The detailed text and lifelike-in-death illustrations caused sensation and outrage.

Subjects for study

Hanged criminals were a source of specimens for dissection. In *The Anatomy Lesson of Dr. Nicolaes Tulp* (1632), by Dutch artist Rembrandt, the dissection subject was robber Aris Kindt. Anatomy lessons were training for physicians and surgeons.

Women and anatomy

Until the 19th century, women in Europe took on only minor medical roles, except as midwives. These Swedish women learning anatomy, in a photograph from about 1880, are probably training for midwifery.

Blade can be sharpened for use

Scalpel

Fine forceps (tweezers)

Needlelike tips

Ridged, splayed tips for gripping

Clamping forceps

Handles have a scissor design.

Fine end

Double-ended small probe

Bulbous end

Hooked point

Hooked needle

Wooden handle

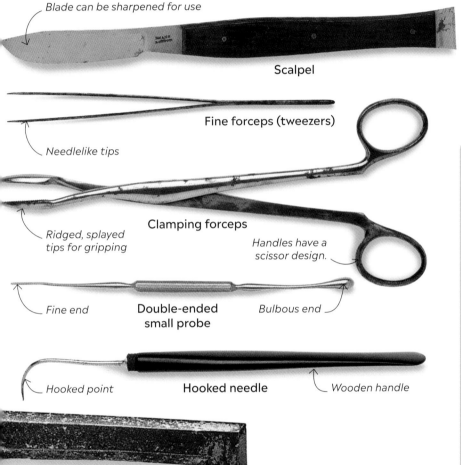

Instruments illustrated in the second edition of Vesalius's book, 1555

Serrated saw blade

Large bone saw

Wooden handle shaped to fit palm of hand

Tensioning screw to tighten blade

👁 EYEWITNESS

Anna Morandi Manzolini

An Italian anatomist and wax modeler, Anna Morandi Manzolini (1714–1774) worked as a lecturer in Bologna, Italy. Along with her husband, she dissected hundreds of corpses to create wax models for teaching anatomy students. Her work helped create a new understanding of the human body.

The microscopic **body**

At the beginning of the 1600s, scientific instrument makers in the Netherlands invented a magnifying device called the microscope. For the first time, scientists used high-quality glass lenses to view objects, illuminated by light, which previously had been far too small to see with the naked eye. Pioneering microscopists showed that living things are made up of much smaller units, which Robert Hooke (1635–1703) likened to the cells, or rooms, of monks in a monastery.

Pioneer histologist

Italy's Marcello Malpighi (1628–1694) was the founder of microscopic anatomy and a pioneer of histology, the study of tissues. He was the first to identify capillaries, the tiny blood vessels that connect arteries to veins.

Lens held between two plates

Pin to hold the specimen in place

Homemade lenses

In the 15th century, most microscopes had two lenses. Dutch scientist Antoni van Leeuwenhoek's simple microscope (left) had one tiny lens, yet it enabled him to observe cells, tissues, and tiny organisms magnified up to 275 times.

Handle to hold the lens close to the eye

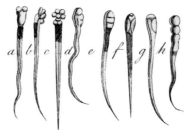

Microscopic drawings

Early microscopists used drawings and writing to record what they had seen. This drawing by van Leeuwenhoek records his observation, for the first time, of sperm cells.

The eyepiece lens magnifies the image produced by the objective lens.

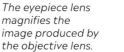

Lens tube

A powerful objective lens collects light from the specimen to create an image.

Stage holds the specimen.

Specimen illuminated with light from below

The lens focuses light rays from the mirror.

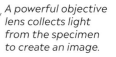

Mirror reflects light from a lamp or window.

Screw adjusts the stage height for focusing.

Tripod base

Compound microscope

Most light microscopes, which use light to illuminate the specimen, are compound, using two or more lenses, as seen in this 19th-century example. This model has the basic features found on a modern compound microscope.

👁 **EYEWITNESS**

Antoni van Leeuwenhoek

Self-taught scientist Antoni van Leeuwenhoek (1632–1723) made about 400 microscopes and helped establish microscopy as a branch of science. He was the first to observe, among many other things, blood cells and sperm as well as bacteria.

Inside a cell

This cutaway model of a typical human cell shows the parts of a cell that can be seen with an electron microscope. A thin cell membrane surrounds the cell. The jellylike cytoplasm contains organelles (small organs), each with a supporting role. The nucleus, the largest structure within the cell, contains the instructions needed to run the cell.

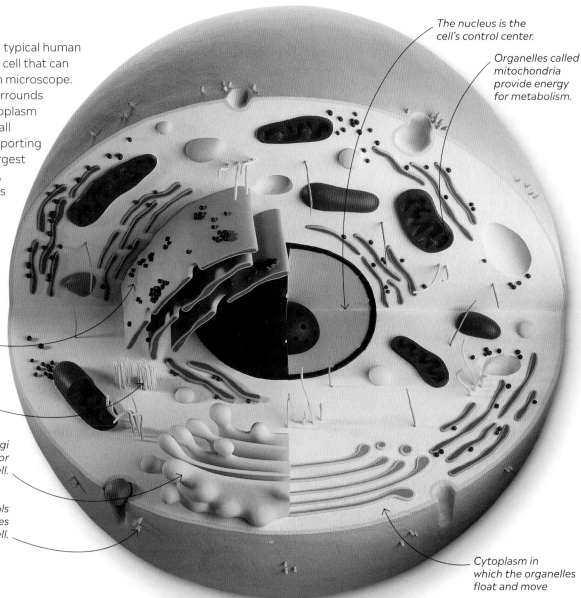

The nucleus is the cell's control center.

Organelles called mitochondria provide energy for metabolism.

Organelles called endoplasmic reticulum transport proteins for cell metabolism.

Microtubule supports and shapes the cell.

Organelle called the Golgi body processes proteins for use inside or outside the cell.

The cell membrane controls the movement of substances in and out of the cell.

Cytoplasm in which the organelles float and move

Electron microscope

An electron microscope uses tiny parts of atoms called electrons to magnify thousands or millions of times. An electron beam is fired toward a specimen at the base. Electrons that pass through or bounce off the specimen are detected and create an image on a monitor.

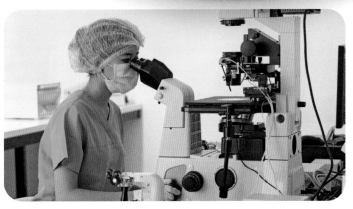

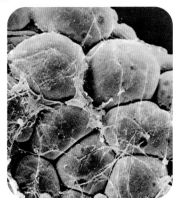

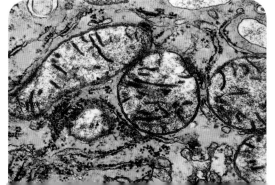

Cell slice

A transmission electron microscope projects an electron beam through a slice of body tissue onto a monitor. The image is photographed to produce a transmission electron micrograph. This TEM shows a liver cell's mitochondria (white) and endoplasmic reticulum (blue).

Surface view

In a scanning electron microscope (SEM), an electron beam scans the surface of a whole specimen. Electrons bouncing off the specimen are focused to create a three-dimensional image. This SEM shows fat cells.

Looking inside
the body

In the past, the only way to see inside the body was to cut it open or inspect wounds. The invention of the ophthalmoscope in 1851 allowed doctors to view the inside of a patient's eye for the first time. In 1895, X-rays were discovered and used to produce images of bones without opening the body. Today's imaging techniques allow us to view tissues, search for signs of disease, and find out how the body works.

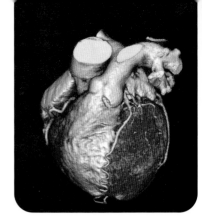

CT scanning

A computed tomography (CT) scan uses X-rays and a computer to look inside the body. A rotating scanner sends a narrow beam of X-rays through the human body to a detector. The result is a two-dimensional slice of the body showing hard and soft tissues. A computer combines image slices together to build a three-dimensional picture of a body part.

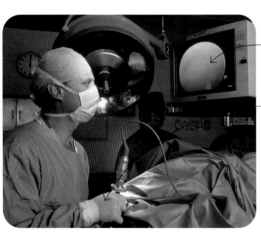

Inside of body is visible on the monitor.

Surgeon moves the endoscope to a new position.

Endoscope

Surgeons use a thin, tubelike endoscope to examine tissues and to look inside joints. It is inserted via a body opening, such as the mouth, or a small incision in the skin (as shown here). Optical fibers inside the tube carry light to illuminate the inside of the body and send back images to a monitor.

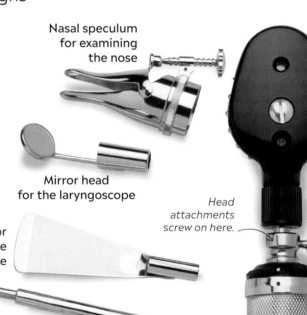

Nasal speculum for examining the nose

Mirror head for the laryngoscope

Head attachments screw on here.

Tongue depressor for the laryngoscope

Laryngoscope head for examining the throat

Otoscope head for examining inside the ear

Video pill

This capsule endoscope can be used to identify damage or disease in the digestive system. It contains a tiny camera, light source, and transmitter. Once swallowed, it travels along the digestive system, taking pictures that are transmitted to an outside receiver.

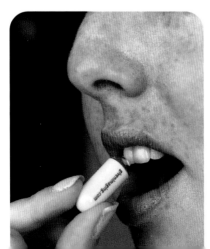

Medical viewing kit

Today's doctors can use this multipurpose medical equipment when examining patients. The kit consists of a handle and a range of attachments used for looking inside the ears, throat, nose, or eyes.

Ophthalmoscope

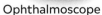

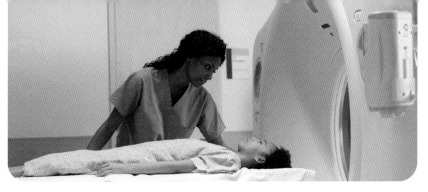

Magnets and radio waves

Inside a magnetic resonance imaging (MRI) scanner, a magnetic field lines up the hydrogen atoms in the body. Bursts of radio waves knock the atoms back into position. When the magnetic field lines the atoms up again, they send out radio signals. Different body parts send differing signals that are detected and turned into images by a computer.

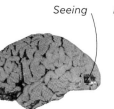
Seeing

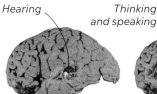
Hearing

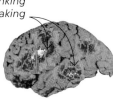
Thinking and speaking

Brain tissue at work

Positron emission tomography (PET) scans reveal how active specific body tissues are. First, a form of glucose (sugar) is injected into the bloodstream to provide food energy for hard-working tissues. As the tissues consume the glucose, particles are released that can be detected to form an image.

Side view of fetus's head

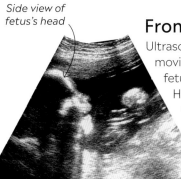

From echo to image

Ultrasound scanning produces moving images, such as this fetus inside the womb. High-pitched sound waves are beamed into the body, reflected back by tissues, and converted into images by a computer.

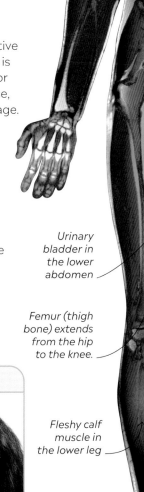

Brain inside the skull

Left lung inside the chest

Urinary bladder in the lower abdomen

Femur (thigh bone) extends from the hip to the knee.

Fleshy calf muscle in the lower leg

Full body scan

This MRI scan shows a vertical cross-section through a man's body. This is produced by combining many individual scans made along the length of the body. The original black-and-white image has been color enhanced to highlight different tissues and organs.

👁 EYEWITNESS

Muyinatu Lediju Bell
U.S. professor Muyinatu Bell is known for her work in groundbreaking medical imaging technology to improve healthcare. She is a part of numerous research centers in the U.S. and has received multiple fellowships and awards. She is the founder and director of the Photoacoustic and Ultrasonic Systems Engineering (PULSE) Lab at Johns Hopkins University.

The body's
framework

Symbol of death

Skeletons are enduring symbols of danger, disease, death, and destruction—as seen in this 15th-century *Dance of Death* drawing.

The skeleton's 206 bones make up a hard yet flexible framework that supports and shapes the body. It surrounds and protects such organs as the brain and heart and keeps them from being jolted or crushed. Bones also anchor the muscles that move the skeleton and, therefore, the whole body. Unlike early anatomists, today's scientists can examine bones inside a living body.

Understanding bones

For centuries, bones were regarded as lifeless supports for the tissues around them. Gradually, anatomists saw that bones were alive, with their own blood vessels and nerves. Here, medieval French surgeon Guy de Chauliac examines a broken bone.

Body mechanics

Many machines copy principles of mechanics shown by the skeleton. For example, each arm has two sets of long bones that can extend the reach of the hand or fold back on themselves—like these cranes.

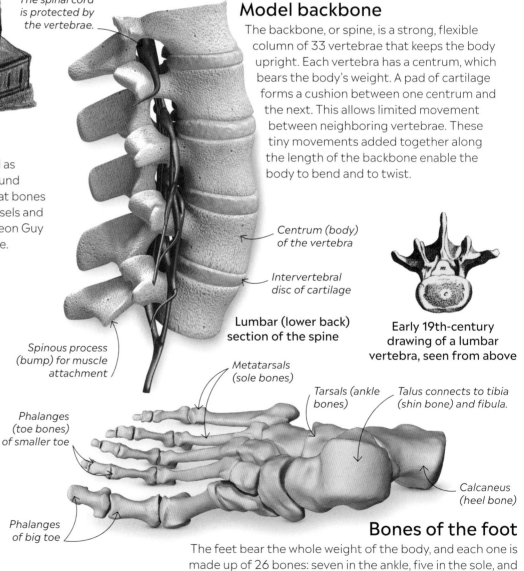

The spinal cord is protected by the vertebrae.

Model backbone

The backbone, or spine, is a strong, flexible column of 33 vertebrae that keeps the body upright. Each vertebra has a centrum, which bears the body's weight. A pad of cartilage forms a cushion between one centrum and the next. This allows limited movement between neighboring vertebrae. These tiny movements added together along the length of the backbone enable the body to bend and to twist.

Centrum (body) of the vertebra

Intervertebral disc of cartilage

Lumbar (lower back) section of the spine

Spinous process (bump) for muscle attachment

Early 19th-century drawing of a lumbar vertebra, seen from above

Metatarsals (sole bones)

Tarsals (ankle bones)

Talus connects to tibia (shin bone) and fibula.

Phalanges (toe bones) of smaller toe

Phalanges of big toe

Calcaneus (heel bone)

Bones of the foot

The feet bear the whole weight of the body, and each one is made up of 26 bones: seven in the ankle, five in the sole, and three in each toe, apart from the big toe, which has two.

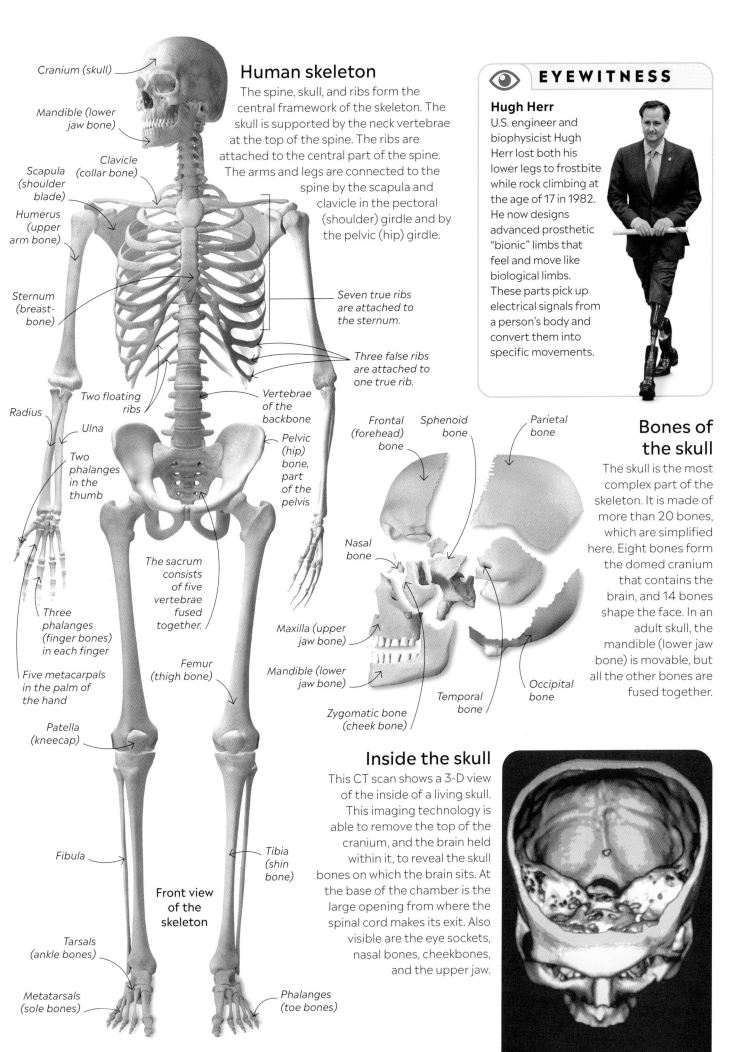

Human skeleton

Cranium (skull)

Mandible (lower jaw bone)

Scapula (shoulder blade)

Clavicle (collar bone)

Humerus (upper arm bone)

Sternum (breast-bone)

Radius

Ulna

Two phalanges in the thumb

Three phalanges (finger bones) in each finger

Five metacarpals in the palm of the hand

Patella (kneecap)

Fibula

Tarsals (ankle bones)

Metatarsals (sole bones)

The spine, skull, and ribs form the central framework of the skeleton. The skull is supported by the neck vertebrae at the top of the spine. The ribs are attached to the central part of the spine. The arms and legs are connected to the spine by the scapula and clavicle in the pectoral (shoulder) girdle and by the pelvic (hip) girdle.

Seven true ribs are attached to the sternum.

Three false ribs are attached to one true rib.

Vertebrae of the backbone

Pelvic (hip) bone, part of the pelvis

Two floating ribs

The sacrum consists of five vertebrae fused together.

Femur (thigh bone)

Tibia (shin bone)

Front view of the skeleton

Phalanges (toe bones)

👁 EYEWITNESS

Hugh Herr
U.S. engineer and biophysicist Hugh Herr lost both his lower legs to frostbite while rock climbing at the age of 17 in 1982. He now designs advanced prosthetic "bionic" limbs that feel and move like biological limbs. These parts pick up electrical signals from a person's body and convert them into specific movements.

Bones of the skull

Frontal (forehead) bone

Sphenoid bone

Parietal bone

Nasal bone

Maxilla (upper jaw bone)

Mandible (lower jaw bone)

Zygomatic bone (cheek bone)

Temporal bone

Occipital bone

The skull is the most complex part of the skeleton. It is made of more than 20 bones, which are simplified here. Eight bones form the domed cranium that contains the brain, and 14 bones shape the face. In an adult skull, the mandible (lower jaw bone) is movable, but all the other bones are fused together.

Inside the skull

This CT scan shows a 3-D view of the inside of a living skull. This imaging technology is able to remove the top of the cranium, and the brain held within it, to reveal the skull bones on which the brain sits. At the base of the chamber is the large opening from where the spinal cord makes its exit. Also visible are the eye sockets, nasal bones, cheekbones, and the upper jaw.

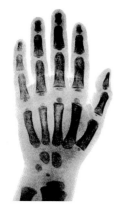

Inside bones

Our bones are living organs, with a complex structure of hard bone tissues, blood vessels, and nerves. Bone is as strong as steel, but only one-sixth its weight. Each bone also has a slight springiness that enables it to withstand knocks and jolts. Tough, dense bony tissue, called compact bone, surrounds light-but-strong spongy bone inside—otherwise the skeleton would be too heavy for the body to move.

Growing bone
In a young embryo, the skeleton forms from bendy cartilage, which then turns into bone over time. This X-ray of a young child's hand shows growing bones (dark blue) and spaces where cartilage will be replaced.

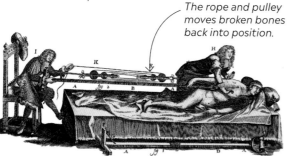

The rope and pulley moves broken bones back into position.

Setting bones
Skeletons of 100,000 years ago show that broken bones were set, or repositioned, to aid healing. Here, 17th-century surgeons are setting a broken arm.

Resisting pressure
When weight is put on a bone, its structure prevents it from bending. For example, in the hip joint (right), the head and neck of the femur (thigh bone) bear the full weight of the body. The largest area of bone consists of spongy bone, in which the trabeculae, or framework of struts, are lined up to resist downward force. The thin covering of compact bone resists squashing on one side of the femur and stretching on the other side.

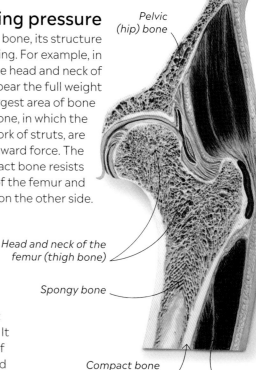

Pelvic (hip) bone

Head and neck of the femur (thigh bone)

Spongy bone

Compact bone resists stretching.

Muscle

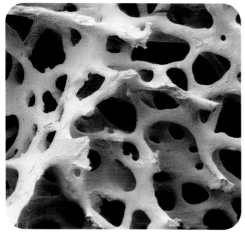

Spongy bone
This SEM of spongy, or cancellous, bone shows an open framework of struts and spaces, or trabeculae. In living bone, these form a structure of great strength, and the spaces are filled with bone marrow. Spongy bone is lighter than compact bone and so reduces the overall weight of a bone.

Inside a long bone
In the cutaway below, compact bone forms the hard outer layer. It is made up of parallel bundles of osteons that run length-wise and act as weight-bearing pillars. Inside is spongy bone and a marrow-filled cavity.

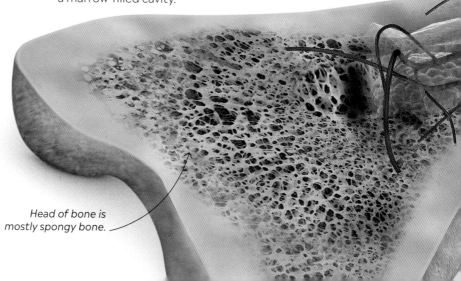

Head of bone is mostly spongy bone.

Bone expert

Italy's Giovanni Ingrassia (1510–1580) was a founder of osteology, or the study of bones. He corrected many mistaken ideas about bones. Ingrassia also identified the body's smallest bone, the stapes of the ear, and described the arrangement of skull bones that form part of the eye socket.

Bone microstructure

This model shows a microscopic view of a slice of compact bone, made up of layered osteons measuring 0.001 in (0.25 mm) wide. Blood vessels run through their central canal, supplying food and oxygen to the bone cells. The bone framework is made of bendy fibers of the protein collagen and hard minerals, mainly calcium phosphate.

Osteon

Osteocyte (bone cell)

Lamellae (layered tubes) of the osteon

Blood vessel

Outer lamellae strengthen the whole bone.

Bone cells

This SEM shows an osteocyte (bone cell) in a lacuna—a tiny space in the framework of minerals and fibers that make up compact bone. Osteocytes are linked by strandlike extensions of their cell bodies that pass along the narrow canals inside bone.

Periosteum

Central canal of the osteon

Branch of blood vessel between the osteons

Spongy bone

Periosteum, a thin, fibrous membrane covering the bone

Head of bone

Bone marrow

Jellylike bone marrow fills the spaces inside spongy bone and the central cavity of long bones. As the body grows, bone-cell-making red marrow is replaced by fat-storing yellow marrow. In adults, red bone marrow remains only in a few bones, such as the skull, spine, and breastbone.

The compact bone is the hard, dense outer layer of the bone.

A rich network of blood vessels nourishes the bone.

Bone shaft

Osteon is one of the layered tubes that make up compact bone.

Central cavity

Veins carry oxygen-poor blood away from the bone cells.

Arteries supply oxygen-rich blood to the bone cells.

Yellow bone marrow fills the central cavity and stores fat.

Making new blood cells

This SEM shows red bone marrow, where blood cells are made. Unspecialized stem cells multiply to produce cells that rapidly multiply again to form billions of red blood cells (red) and white blood cells (blue).

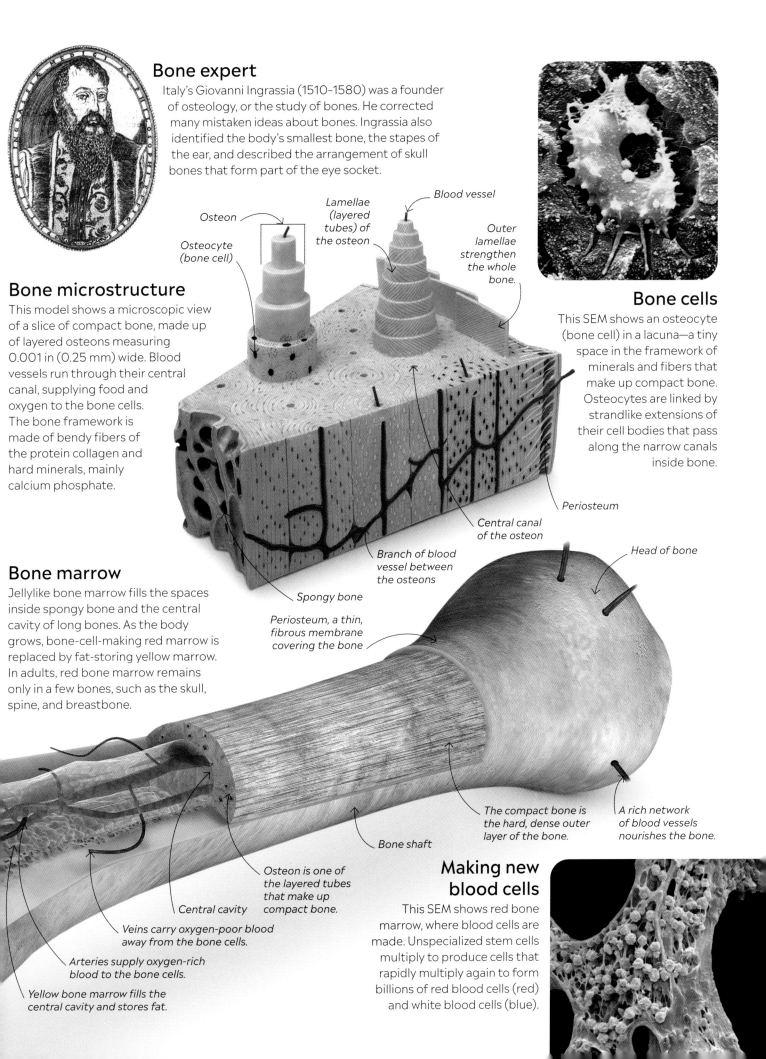

The body's joints

Supple joints
Joints benefit from use and deteriorate with neglect. Activities such as yoga promote the full range of joint movement and ensure maximum flexibility.

Joints galore
With its 27 bones and 19 movable joints, the hand can perform many delicate tasks. The first knuckle joint of each digit (finger) is condyloid—it and the other hinge joints allow the fingers to grasp objects. The saddle joint at the base of the thumb lets it swing across the palm and touch the tips of the other fingers for a grip.

Wherever two or more bones meet in the skeleton, they form a joint. Most of the body's 400-plus joints, such as those in our fingers and toes, are synovial, or freely movable. There are several types of movable joint, held together by ligaments, which makes the skeleton incredibly flexible. Without them, it would be rigid.

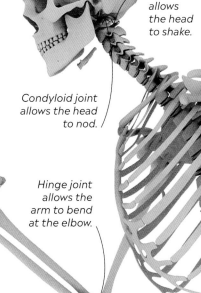

Pivot joint allows the head to shake.

Condyloid joint allows the head to nod.

Hinge joint allows the arm to bend at the elbow.

Ball-and-socket joint in the hip

Limb can move in many directions.

Pelvic (hip) bone

Femur (thigh bone)

Femur (thigh bone)

Hinge joint in the knee

Limb moves back and forth in one direction.

Tibia (shin bone)

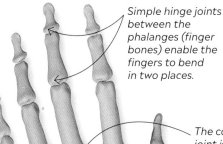

Simple hinge joints between the phalanges (finger bones) enable the fingers to bend in two places.

The condyloid joint is an oval ball-and-socket joint allowing the fingers to swivel, but not to rotate.

Palm of hand extends to the knuckles.

Saddle joint gives thumb flexibility and a delicate touch when picking up tiny objects with the finger.

Gliding joints allow sliding movements between the eight bones of the wrist.

Balls, sockets, and hinges
The hip's and knee's movements can be seen when a person moves. The hip joint is a ball-and-socket joint. The rounded end of the thigh bone swivels in the cup-shaped socket in the hip bone and permits movement in all directions. The knee is a hinge joint and moves mainly in a front-to-back direction.

A gliding joint allows the kneecap to move away from the femur (thigh bone) as the knee bends.

Hinge joint allows the foot to bend at the ankle

Versatile mover
The skeleton is very flexible because it has different types of joint, permitting different ranges of movement. Ball-and-socket, condyloid, and saddle joints allow flexible movements in several directions. Pivot joints allow movement from side to side, hinge joints go back and forth, and gliding joints allow small sliding movements between bones.

Binding the bones

Tough straps of strong, elastic tissue called ligaments surround bone ends in a joint—such as the ankle—and bind them together securely to prevent them from moving excessively.

Tibia (shin bone)

Fibula

Ligament linking the calcaneus and fibula

Calcaneus (heel bone)

Pivot joint permits the forearm to twist.

Gliding joint between the rib and backbone

Saddle joint gives the thumb great mobility.

Condyloid joint gives the wrist flexibility.

A ball-and-socket joint between the femur (thigh bone) and hip enables the leg to move in all directions.

Hinge joint allows the leg to bend at the knee.

The gliding joint between the tarsals (ankle bones) allows little movement, which strengthens the ankle.

Condyloid joint allows the toes to bend and wiggle.

Hinge joint allows the toe to bend.

Ligament linking the tibia and fibula

Tarsal (ankle bone)

Ligaments connecting the tarsals and metatarsals

Metatarsals (sole bones)

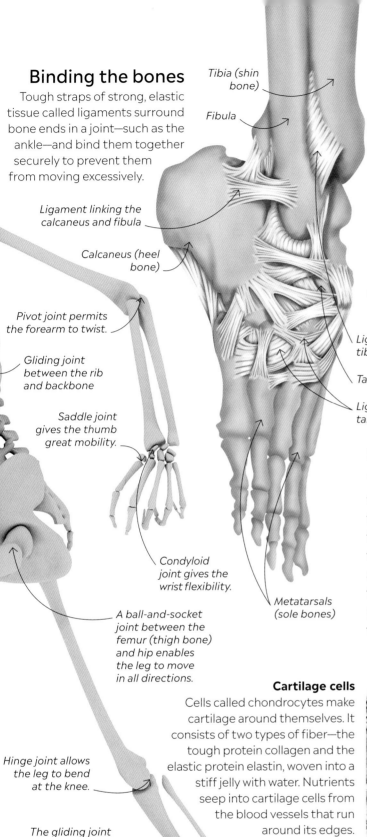

Inside a synovial joint

This image shows the main parts of a typical, movable joint. Inside the joint capsule and ligaments is the synovial membrane. This makes synovial fluid, the oil that lubricates the joint. The bone ends are covered by friction-reducing, shiny hyaline cartilage.

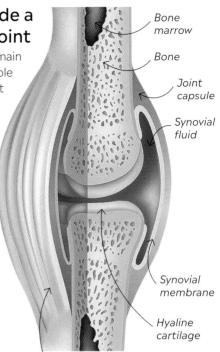

Bone marrow

Bone

Joint capsule

Synovial fluid

Synovial membrane

Hyaline cartilage

Ligaments

Cartilage

Tough and flexible, cartilage is a supporting tissue that resists pushing and pulling forces. There are three types. Hyaline cartilage covers bone ends to help joints move smoothly. It also connects the ribs to the sternum. Elastic cartilage is strong and stretchy. It supports the outside of the ear, for example. Fibrocartilage can withstand heavy pressure and is found in the discs between vertebrae in the backbone and in the knee joints.

Cartilage cells

Cells called chondrocytes make cartilage around themselves. It consists of two types of fiber—the tough protein collagen and the elastic protein elastin, woven into a stiff jelly with water. Nutrients seep into cartilage cells from the blood vessels that run around its edges.

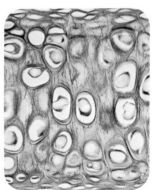

Knee trouble

The knee is the body's biggest joint. It is strengthened by ligaments inside the joint and cushioned from jolts by pads of cartilage called the menisci. Sports such as soccer involve rapid turns and high kicks, which can cause knee injuries.

21

Muscle **power**

Muscle tissue pulls—and generates movement—by contracting, or getting shorter. Skeletal muscles make up nearly half the body's total mass. They shape the body and, by pulling on bones, hold it upright to maintain posture and allow it to perform a wide range of movements from blinking to running. The two other muscle types are smooth and cardiac muscle. Most muscles have Latin names that describe their location, size, shape, or action.

Under the microscope

Danish bishop Nicholas Steno (1638–1686) looked at muscles with a microscope and found that their contraction was due to the combined shortening of the thousands of tiny fibers that make up each muscle.

INSIDE A SKELETAL MUSCLE

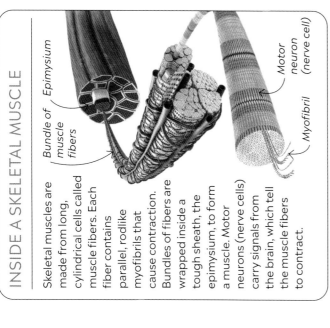

Skeletal muscles are made from long, cylindrical cells called muscle fibers. Each fiber contains parallel, rodlike myofibrils that cause contraction. Bundles of fibers are wrapped inside a tough sheath, the epimysium, to form a muscle. Motor neurons (nerve cells) carry signals from the brain, which tell the muscle fibers to contract.

Epimysium

Bundle of muscle fibers

Motor neuron (nerve cell)

Myofibril

Muscles make up 40 percent of the weight of the human body.

Semispinalis capitis tilts the head to look up.

Trapezius acts to brace the shoulders and pull back the head.

Latissimus dorsi pulls the arm backward and downward.

Deltoid raises the arm away from the body, to the side, front, or rear.

Infraspinatus rotates the arm outward.

Erector spinae straightens the back.

Sternocleidomastoid tilts the head.

Pectoralis major pulls the arm in and rotates it.

Pectoralis minor pulls the shoulder downward.

Biceps brachii bends the elbow.

Rectus abdominis muscles on either side of the navel tense to hold in a flabby belly.

Masseter closes an open jaw.

Intercostal muscles move the ribs in breathing.

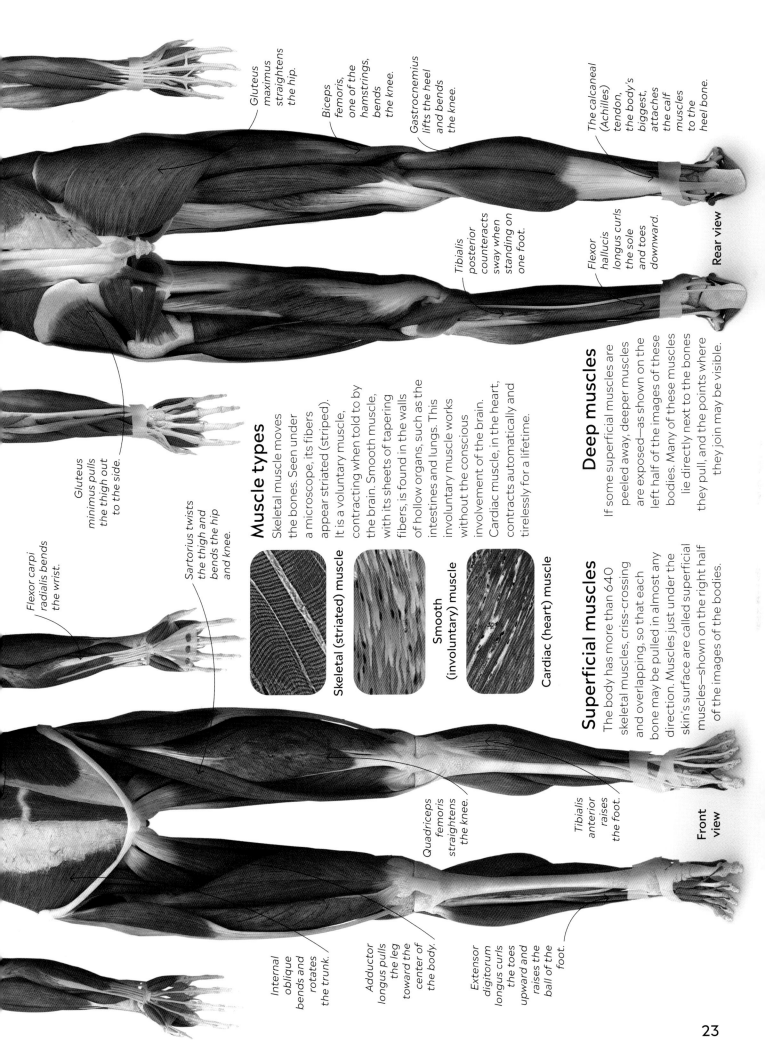

Gluteus maximus straightens the hip.

Biceps femoris, one of the hamstrings, bends the knee.

Gastrocnemius lifts the heel and bends the knee.

The calcaneal (Achilles) tendon, the body's biggest, attaches the calf muscles to the heel bone.

Tibialis posterior counteracts sway when standing on one foot.

Flexor hallucis longus curls the sole and toes downward.

Rear view

Gluteus minimus pulls the thigh out to the side.

Flexor carpi radialis bends the wrist.

Sartorius twists the thigh and bends the hip and knee.

Muscle types

Skeletal muscle moves the bones. Seen under a microscope, its fibers appear striated (striped). It is a voluntary muscle, contracting when told to by the brain. Smooth muscle, with its sheets of tapering fibers, is found in the walls of hollow organs, such as the intestines and lungs. This involuntary muscle works without the conscious involvement of the brain. Cardiac muscle, in the heart, contracts automatically and tirelessly for a lifetime.

Skeletal (striated) muscle

Smooth (involuntary) muscle

Cardiac (heart) muscle

Deep muscles

If some superficial muscles are peeled away, deeper muscles are exposed—as shown on the left half of the images of these bodies. Many of these muscles lie directly next to the bones they pull, and the points where they join may be visible.

Superficial muscles

The body has more than 640 skeletal muscles, criss-crossing and overlapping, so that each bone may be pulled in almost any direction. Muscles just under the skin's surface are called superficial muscles—shown on the right half of the images of the bodies.

Quadriceps femoris straightens the knee.

Tibialis anterior raises the foot.

Front view

Internal oblique bends and rotates the trunk.

Adductor longus pulls the leg toward the center of the body.

Extensor digitorum longus curls the toes upward and raises the ball of the foot.

The moving body

Muscles are attached to bones by tough, fibrous cords called tendons. When muscles contract (get shorter), they pull on a bone. The bone that moves when the muscle contracts is called the insertion, and the other bone, which stays still, is called the origin. Muscles can only pull, not push, so moving a body part in different directions requires opposing pairs of muscles.

Muscles in the back of the forearm extend (straighten) the fingers.

Neck muscles bend the head back.

Muscles at the back of the thigh pull the leg backward.

Back muscles arch the back.

The three S-words

Muscle fitness can be assessed by strength, stamina, and suppleness. Swimming and dancing promote all three.

Working together

To perform this pose, areas of the brain that control movement and balance send out nerve signals to instruct specific skeletal muscles when to contract and by how much. Muscles in the body work together to put the dancer in this position. Signals from the muscles and tendons also feed back to the brain so that minor adjustments maintain her balance.

Muscle at the front of the thigh pulls the leg forward and straightens the knee.

Pairs of muscles at the front and back of the leg tense to keep balance.

Triceps contracted

Biceps relaxed

Elbow straight

Biceps contracted

Forearm lowered

Triceps relaxed

Raised forearm

Flexed elbow

Muscle pairs

Muscles can only contract and pull, so moving a body part in opposite directions requires two different muscles. Many muscles are arranged in opposing pairs. In the arm, the biceps pulls the forearm upward and bends the elbow, while its opposing partner, the triceps, pulls the forearm downward and straightens the elbow.

Tendons

Many of the muscles that move the fingers are not in the hand but in the forearm. They work the fingers by remote control, using long tendons extending from the ends of the muscles to attach to the bones that they move. The tendons run smoothly in slippery tendon sheaths that reduce wear.

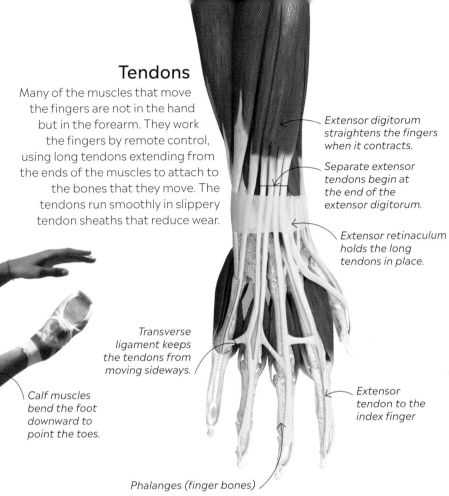

Extensor digitorum straightens the fingers when it contracts.

Separate extensor tendons begin at the end of the extensor digitorum.

Extensor retinaculum holds the long tendons in place.

Transverse ligament keeps the tendons from moving sideways.

Extensor tendon to the index finger

Phalanges (finger bones)

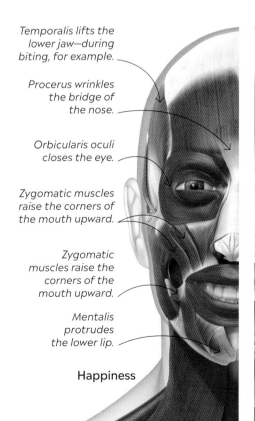

Calf muscles bend the foot downward to point the toes.

Power and precision

With practice, pianists can train their brains to coordinate complex, rhythmic movements in all 10 fingers. Muscles work the flexible framework of 27 bones in each hand to play notes ranging from delicate to explosive.

Face, head, and neck

From frowning to smiling, around 30 facial muscles produce the great variety of expressions. These muscles are also involved in such activities as blinking and chewing. They work by joining the skull bones to different areas of skin, which are tugged as the muscles contract. The head is supported and moved by muscles that start at the backbone, shoulder blades, and bones in the upper chest.

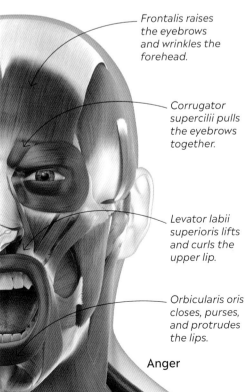

Temporalis lifts the lower jaw—during biting, for example.

Procerus wrinkles the bridge of the nose.

Orbicularis oculi closes the eye.

Zygomatic muscles raise the corners of the mouth upward.

Zygomatic muscles raise the corners of the mouth upward.

Mentalis protrudes the lower lip.

Happiness

Frontalis raises the eyebrows and wrinkles the forehead.

Corrugator supercilii pulls the eyebrows together.

Levator labii superioris lifts and curls the upper lip.

Orbicularis oris closes, purses, and protrudes the lips.

Anger

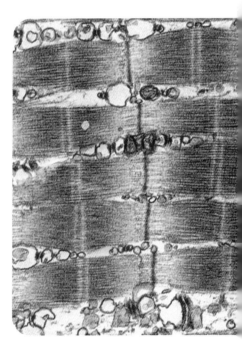

Myofibril contraction

This image shows myofibrils— long cylinders that extend the length of a skeletal muscle fiber, or cell. They are divided into units—each containing thick and thin filaments, producing the blue-and-pink pattern. The filaments slide over each other, making the myofibril—and the entire muscle—shorter.

The nervous system

With split-second timing, our nervous system allows us to feel, see, hear, move, and think and remember—all at the same time. It also automatically controls many internal body processes that we are unaware of, such as the body's heart rate. It is run by the brain and spinal cord, which form the central nervous system (CNS) and link to the body's network of nerves.

Nerve network

The brain and spinal cord form the control center of a network of nerves. Nerves are bundles of interconnected neuron cells and divide to reach all the body's tissues.

Facial nerve controls the muscles of facial expression.

Trigeminal nerve branch supplies the upper teeth and cheek.

Founder of neurology

French physician Jean-Martin Charcot (1825–1893) was a pioneer of neurology, the study of nervous system diseases, and of psychiatry, the branch of medicine that deals with mental illness.

Cranial and spinal nerves

The brain—the cerebrum, cerebellum, and brain stem—and the spinal cord function through a constant flow of signals. These arrive and depart through 12 pairs of cranial nerves that start in the brain and 31 pairs of spinal nerves that start in the spinal cord. Most nerves have sensory neurons, which carry sensations from a body area to the brain, and motor neurons, which carry instructions from the brain to move muscles in that same area.

Brachial plexus leads to the nerves that supply the arm and hand.

Ulnar nerve controls the muscles that bend the wrist and fingers.

Intercostal nerve controls the muscles between the ribs.

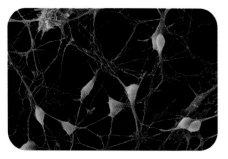

Branches everywhere

These are association neurons in the brain. Each has branching links with thousands of other neurons, forming a communication network with countless routes for nerve signals.

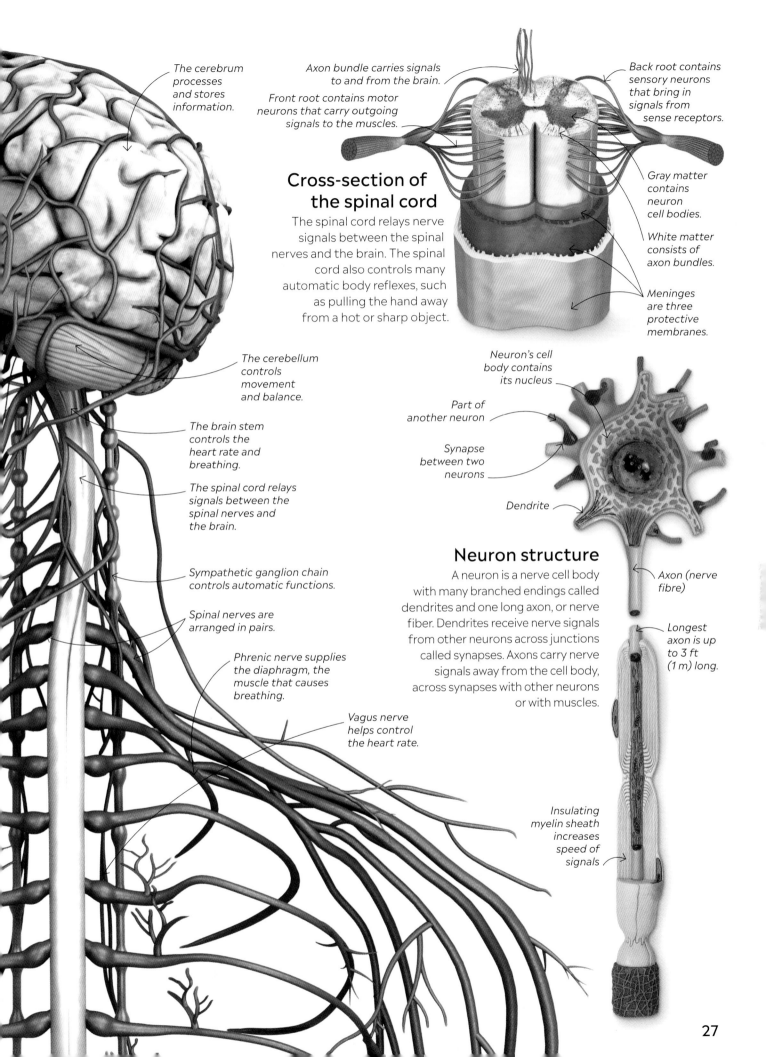

The cerebrum processes and stores information.

Axon bundle carries signals to and from the brain.

Front root contains motor neurons that carry outgoing signals to the muscles.

Back root contains sensory neurons that bring in signals from sense receptors.

Cross-section of the spinal cord

The spinal cord relays nerve signals between the spinal nerves and the brain. The spinal cord also controls many automatic body reflexes, such as pulling the hand away from a hot or sharp object.

Gray matter contains neuron cell bodies.

White matter consists of axon bundles.

Meninges are three protective membranes.

The cerebellum controls movement and balance.

The brain stem controls the heart rate and breathing.

The spinal cord relays signals between the spinal nerves and the brain.

Sympathetic ganglion chain controls automatic functions.

Spinal nerves are arranged in pairs.

Phrenic nerve supplies the diaphragm, the muscle that causes breathing.

Vagus nerve helps control the heart rate.

Neuron's cell body contains its nucleus

Part of another neuron

Synapse between two neurons

Dendrite

Neuron structure

A neuron is a nerve cell body with many branched endings called dendrites and one long axon, or nerve fiber. Dendrites receive nerve signals from other neurons across junctions called synapses. Axons carry nerve signals away from the cell body, across synapses with other neurons or with muscles.

Axon (nerve fibre)

Longest axon is up to 3 ft (1 m) long.

Insulating myelin sheath increases speed of signals

27

The brain

The brain is our most complex organ and our nervous system's control center. It contains 100 billion neurons (nerve cells), each linked to hundreds or thousands of other neurons, which together form a vast communication network with incredible processing power. Over the past two centuries, scientists have mapped the brain and how it works.

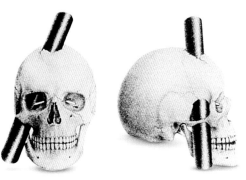

Hole in the head

Phineas Gage worked in a quarry in Vermont. In 1848, a gunpowder accident blew a metal rod through the left frontal lobe of his brain. Gage survived, but he changed from contented and polite to moody and foul-mouthed—living proof that the front of the brain is involved in personality.

The brain from below

The brain has three main parts. The cerebrum makes up 85 percent of its weight. It processes and stores incoming information and sends out instructions to the body. The brain stem relays signals between the cerebrum and the spinal cord and controls automatic functions, such as the heart rate and breathing. The cerebellum is responsible for controlling balance and posture and for coordinating movements.

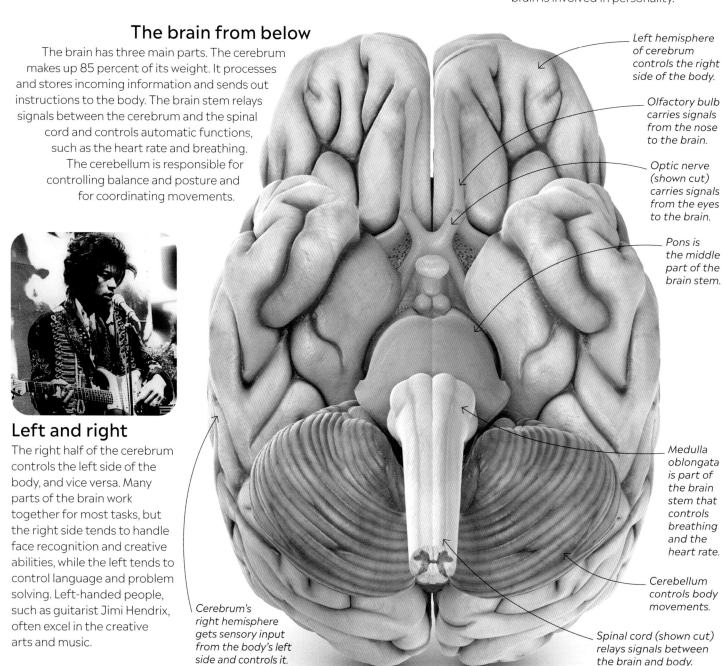

Left hemisphere of cerebrum controls the right side of the body.

Olfactory bulb carries signals from the nose to the brain.

Optic nerve (shown cut) carries signals from the eyes to the brain.

Pons is the middle part of the brain stem.

Medulla oblongata is part of the brain stem that controls breathing and the heart rate.

Cerebellum controls body movements.

Spinal cord (shown cut) relays signals between the brain and body.

Cerebrum's right hemisphere gets sensory input from the body's left side and controls it.

Left and right

The right half of the cerebrum controls the left side of the body, and vice versa. Many parts of the brain work together for most tasks, but the right side tends to handle face recognition and creative abilities, while the left tends to control language and problem solving. Left-handed people, such as guitarist Jimi Hendrix, often excel in the creative arts and music.

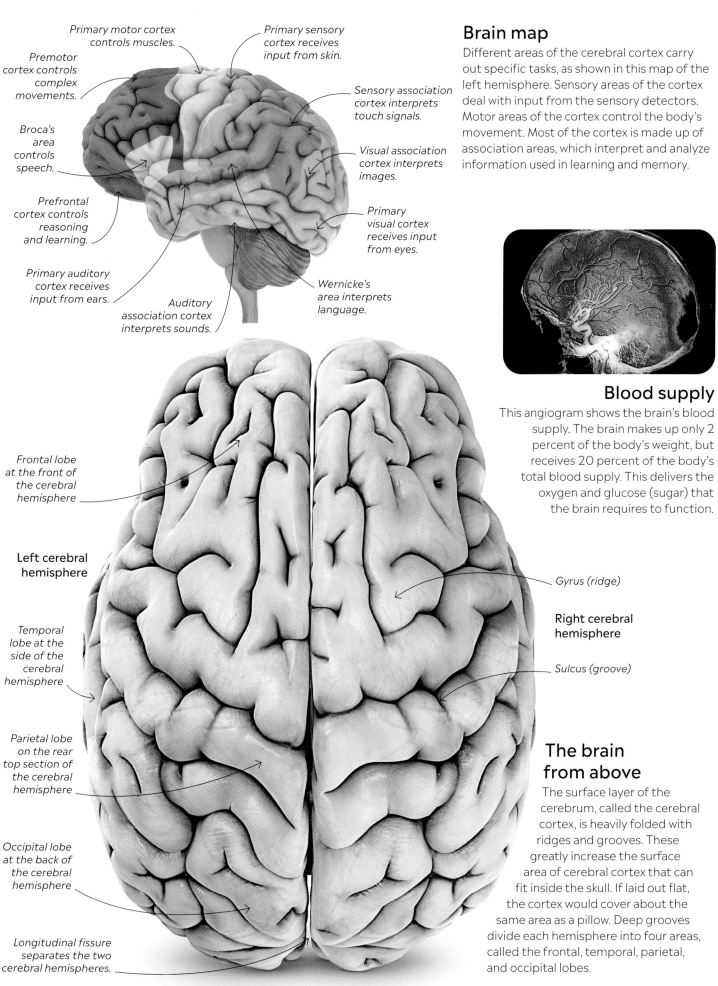

Primary motor cortex controls muscles.

Primary sensory cortex receives input from skin.

Premotor cortex controls complex movements.

Sensory association cortex interprets touch signals.

Broca's area controls speech.

Visual association cortex interprets images.

Prefrontal cortex controls reasoning and learning.

Primary visual cortex receives input from eyes.

Primary auditory cortex receives input from ears.

Auditory association cortex interprets sounds.

Wernicke's area interprets language.

Brain map

Different areas of the cerebral cortex carry out specific tasks, as shown in this map of the left hemisphere. Sensory areas of the cortex deal with input from the sensory detectors. Motor areas of the cortex control the body's movement. Most of the cortex is made up of association areas, which interpret and analyze information used in learning and memory.

Blood supply

This angiogram shows the brain's blood supply. The brain makes up only 2 percent of the body's weight, but receives 20 percent of the body's total blood supply. This delivers the oxygen and glucose (sugar) that the brain requires to function.

Frontal lobe at the front of the cerebral hemisphere

Left cerebral hemisphere

Temporal lobe at the side of the cerebral hemisphere

Parietal lobe on the rear top section of the cerebral hemisphere

Occipital lobe at the back of the cerebral hemisphere

Longitudinal fissure separates the two cerebral hemispheres.

Gyrus (ridge)

Right cerebral hemisphere

Sulcus (groove)

The brain from above

The surface layer of the cerebrum, called the cerebral cortex, is heavily folded with ridges and grooves. These greatly increase the surface area of cerebral cortex that can fit inside the skull. If laid out flat, the cortex would cover about the same area as a pillow. Deep grooves divide each hemisphere into four areas, called the frontal, temporal, parietal, and occipital lobes.

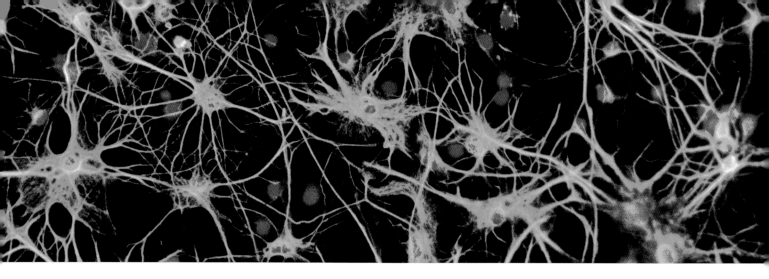

Inside the **brain**

Deep inside the brain, the thalamus acts as a relay station for incoming nerve signals, and the hypothalamus automatically controls a vast array of body activities. The limbic system is the emotional center of the brain, dealing with instincts, fears, and feelings. Inside the cerebrum, linked chambers called ventricles are filled with cerebrospinal fluid (CSF). CSF is produced by blood and circulates through the ventricles, helping feed the brain cells.

Sweet dreams
French artist Henri Rousseau (1844-1910) painted a musician dreaming about a lion in *The Sleeping Gypsy*. While we sleep, the brain replays recent experiences at random and stores significant events in the memory. Dreaming is a side effect of this activity.

Midbrain is at the top of the brain stem.

Thalamus relays nerve signals to the cerebrum.

Inner surface of the left cerebral hemisphere

The corpus callosum (band of nerve fibers) connects the left and right cerebral hemispheres.

Ventricle contains cerebrospinal fluid to feed the brain cells.

The hypothalamus controls many automatic activities, including sleep.

Cerebellum controls muscle movement and balance.

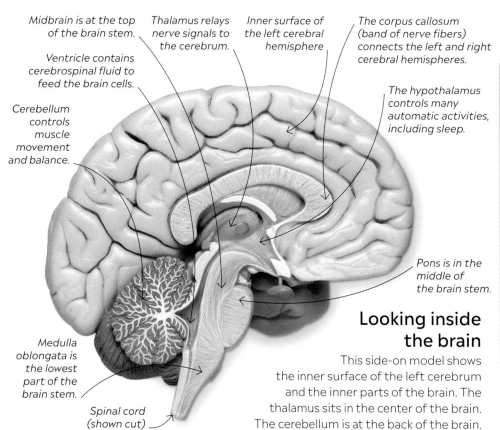

Medulla oblongata is the lowest part of the brain stem.

Spinal cord (shown cut)

Pons is in the middle of the brain stem.

Looking inside the brain
This side-on model shows the inner surface of the left cerebrum and the inner parts of the brain. The thalamus sits in the center of the brain. The cerebellum is at the back of the brain.

EYEWITNESS

Sigmund Freud
Austrian physician Sigmund Freud (1856-1939) developed his technique of psychoanalysis, in which patients talk freely about their personal experiences. He believed that many mental disorders can be treated by investigating the unconscious mind.

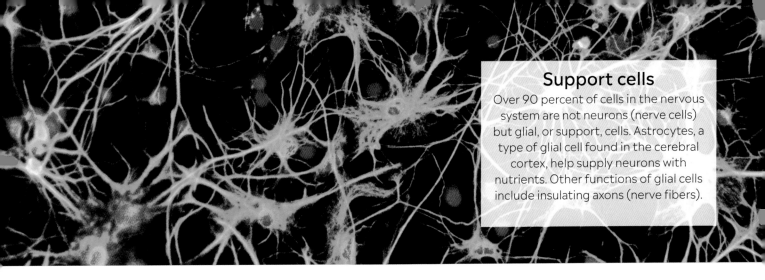

Support cells

Over 90 percent of cells in the nervous system are not neurons (nerve cells) but glial, or support, cells. Astrocytes, a type of glial cell found in the cerebral cortex, help supply neurons with nutrients. Other functions of glial cells include insulating axons (nerve fibers).

The limbic system

A curve of linked structures is located on the inner surface of each cerebral hemisphere and around the top of the brain stem. It deals with emotions and helps us store memories. As the sense of smell is linked to the limbic system, certain odors can trigger memories.

Meditation

Scientists continue to explore how the brain works. Some people look beyond its nerve signals and believe that such techniques as meditation can carry the mind beyond the physical boundaries of the body.

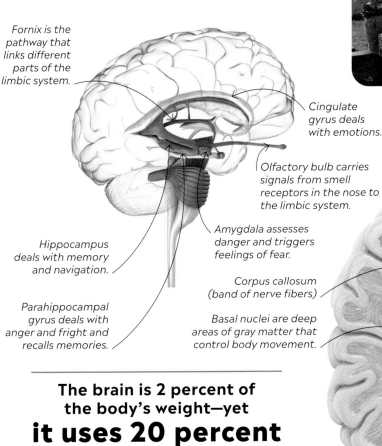

Fornix is the pathway that links different parts of the limbic system.

Cingulate gyrus deals with emotions.

Olfactory bulb carries signals from smell receptors in the nose to the limbic system.

Hippocampus deals with memory and navigation.

Amygdala assesses danger and triggers feelings of fear.

Parahippocampal gyrus deals with anger and fright and recalls memories.

Corpus callosum (band of nerve fibers)

Basal nuclei are deep areas of gray matter that control body movement.

The brain is 2 percent of the body's weight—yet it uses 20 percent of its energy.

Gray and white matter

This vertical cross-section shows a front view of the cerebrum. The cerebral cortex is made of gray matter. This consists of neuron cell bodies, dendrites, and short axons. White matter consists of longer axons, which join parts of the cerebral cortex together, or connect the brain to the rest of the nervous system.

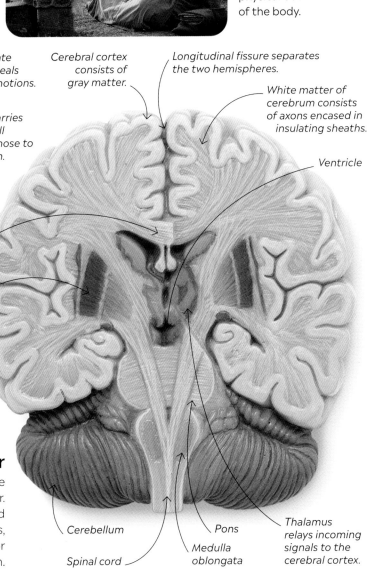

Cerebral cortex consists of gray matter.

Longitudinal fissure separates the two hemispheres.

White matter of cerebrum consists of axons encased in insulating sheaths.

Ventricle

Cerebellum

Pons

Medulla oblongata

Spinal cord

Thalamus relays incoming signals to the cerebral cortex.

Skin and **touch**

As well as its role in the sense of touch, skin has many other jobs. Its tough surface layer, the epidermis, keeps out water, dust, germs, and harmful ultraviolet rays from the sun. Underneath is a thicker layer, the dermis, which is packed with sensory receptors, nerves, and blood vessels. It helps steady our body temperature at 98.6°F (37°C) by releasing sweat. Hair and nails provide additional body covering and protection.

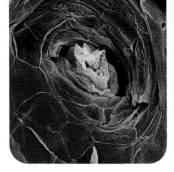

Cooling the body
This is one of about three million sweat pores in the skin's surface. When sweat glands in the dermis release sweat through the pores, the process draws heat from the body and cools it down.

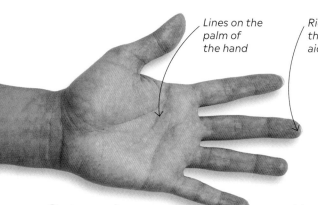

Lines on the palm of the hand

Ridges on the fingertips aid grip.

Light touch and pressure receptor

Epidermis consists of several layers.

Lowest layer of the epidermis replaces surface cells.

Hair

Sebaceous gland releases sebum through the hair follicle.

Temperature or pain receptor

Upper layer of the epidermis

Sweat pore

Get a grip
The skin on the palm of the hand is covered with ridges. These help the hand grip objects when performing different tasks. Beneath the palm, a triangle-shaped sheet of tough, meshed fibers anchors the skin and stops it from sliding over the underlying fat and muscle.

Under your skin
The upper surface of the epidermis consists of dead cells filled with keratin. The skin flakes as dead cells wear away and are replaced with new ones produced in the lowest layer of the epidermis. The thicker dermis layer contains the sense receptors that help the body detect changes in temperature, touch, vibration, pressure, and pain. The dermis also houses coiled sweat glands and hair follicles. Oily sebum keeps the skin and hair soft and flexible.

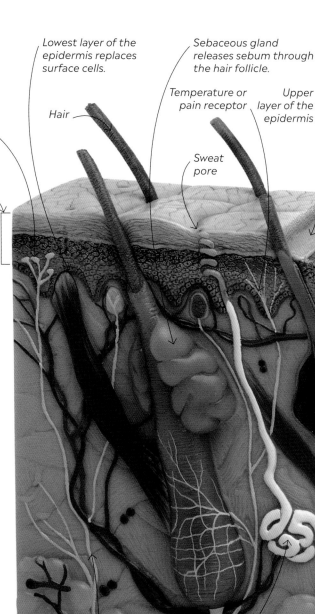

Nerve carries signals to the brain.

Sweat gland

 EYEWITNESS

Louis Braille
French educator Louis Braille (1809–1852) was blinded when he was three years old. In 1824, he devised a system in which patterns of raised dots that represented letters and numbers could be felt through the fingertips. This enabled people with sight problems to read.

Loop pattern on fingerprint

Fingerprints

The skin on the fingers, toes, palms, and soles is folded into swirling patterns of tiny ridges. The ridges help this skin grip, aided by sweat released through pores along each ridge. When fingers touch smooth surfaces, such as glass, their ridges leave behind sweaty patterns, or prints. Each human has a unique set of fingerprints.

Nail growth

A typical fingernail grows about 0.12 in (3 mm) in a month. Fingernails also grow faster in summer than in winter. Toenails grow three or four times more slowly.

Uncut fingernails curl as they grow.

INSENSITIVE NAILS

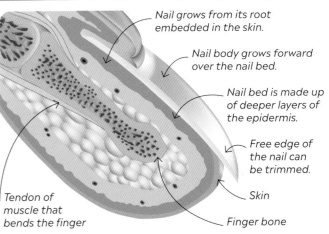

Nail grows from its root embedded in the skin.

Nail body grows forward over the nail bed.

Nail bed is made up of deeper layers of the epidermis.

Free edge of the nail can be trimmed.

Skin

Finger bone

Tendon of muscle that bends the finger

Nails protect the ends of fingers and toes. They are hard extensions of the epidermis, made from dead cells filled with keratin. Each nail grows from new cells produced in the root. These push the nail body forward over the nail bed as it grows.

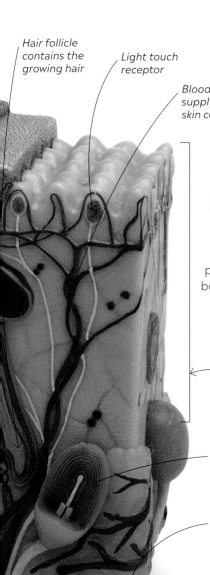

Hair follicle contains the growing hair

Light touch receptor

Blood vessels supply the skin cells.

The dermis is firmly attached to the epidermis.

Pressure and vibration receptor

Fat layer under the dermis insulates the body

Fingertips are packed with touch receptors.

Tongue and lips are very sensitive.

Face has sensitive areas.

A sensitive body

Different parts of the body have varying numbers of sense receptors in the skin for detecting touch, pressure, and vibration. This body is exaggerated to show which areas of skin have the most and are therefore most sensitive to touch.

Dead hairs

These hair shafts in the skin grow from living cells at the base of the follicle. As the cells push upward, they fill with keratin and die. Short, fine hairs cover much of the body. Longer, thicker hairs protect the scalp from harmful sunlight and prevent heat loss.

Skin color

Skin color depends on how much melanin, or brown pigment (coloring), it contains. Melanin is produced by cells in the lowest layer of the epidermis. It protects against the harmful, ultraviolet rays in sunlight, which can damage skin cells and the tissues underneath.

Eyes and **seeing**

The eyes contain more than 70 percent of the body's sensory receptors, in the form of light-detecting cells. Our eyes move automatically, adjust to dim and bright light, and focus light from objects near or far. This light is turned into electrical signals, sent to the brain, and changed into the images we see.

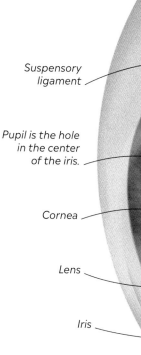

Fovea

Suspensory ligament

Pupil is the hole in the center of the iris.

Cornea

Lens

Iris

Ciliary muscles

Sclera

Cross-eyed

This Arabic drawing, nearly 1,000 years old, shows the optic nerves. Half of the nerve fibers from the right eye pass to the left side of the brain, and vice versa.

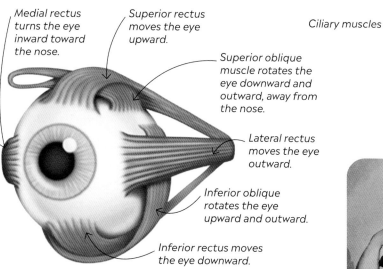

Medial rectus turns the eye inward toward the nose.

Superior rectus moves the eye upward.

Superior oblique muscle rotates the eye downward and outward, away from the nose.

Lateral rectus moves the eye outward.

Inferior oblique rotates the eye upward and outward.

Inferior rectus moves the eye downward.

Moving the eye

Eyeballs swivel in their sockets to follow moving objects. They also make tiny, jumping movements when scanning the words on this page. Just six slim muscles produce all these movements.

Eyelids and tears

Tears are produced by a lacrimal (tear) gland behind each upper eyelid and flow along ducts to be spread over the eye with each blink. Tears keep the eye moist and wash away dust. Used tear fluid drains away through two holes in the lower eyelids and along two ducts into the nose.

Outer layers

The wall of the eyeball has three layers. Outermost is the tough sclera, visible at the front as the white of the eye, except where the clear cornea allows light in. Next is the choroid, filled with blood vessels that supply the other two layers. The innermost layer is the retina. Millions of light-detecting cells at the back of the retina send image information to the brain.

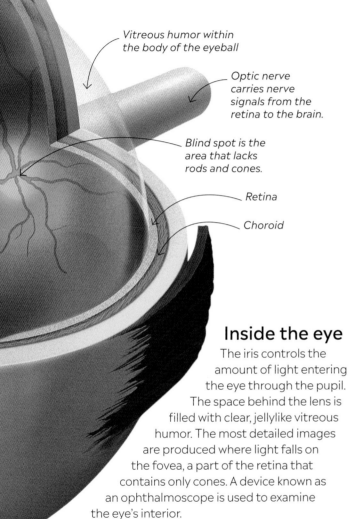

Vitreous humor within the body of the eyeball

Optic nerve carries nerve signals from the retina to the brain.

Blind spot is the area that lacks rods and cones.

Retina

Choroid

Eyes forward

Only one-sixth of an eyeball can be seen from the outside. The rest sits within a deep bowl of skull bone, the eye socket. Eyebrows, eyelids, and eyelashes protect the front of the eye by shading it from dust, sweat, and excessive light. The color of the iris depends on the amount of melanin present.

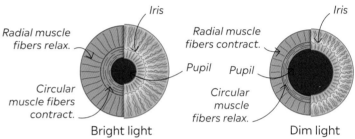

Radial muscle fibers relax.

Iris

Circular muscle fibers contract.

Pupil

Bright light

Radial muscle fibers contract.

Iris

Pupil

Circular muscle fibers relax.

Dim light

Pupil size

Muscle fibers (red) in the iris adjust the size of the pupil automatically. To avoid dazzle in bright light, circular fibers contract to make the pupil smaller. In dim light, to let more in, radial fibers contract to enlarge the pupil.

Inside the eye

The iris controls the amount of light entering the eye through the pupil. The space behind the lens is filled with clear, jellylike vitreous humor. The most detailed images are produced where light falls on the fovea, a part of the retina that contains only cones. A device known as an ophthalmoscope is used to examine the eye's interior.

Rods and cones

The retina has two kinds of light-detecting cells. The rods (green) see only in shades of gray but respond well in dim light. The cones (blue) are mainly at the back of the retina and see details and colors but work well only in bright light.

FORMING AN IMAGE

When we look at an object, light rays reflected from that object are partly focused, or bent, by the cornea. The light then passes through the pupil to the lens, which projects a sharp upside-down image onto the retina. It sends nerve signals along the optic nerve to the brain, which turns the image the right way up.

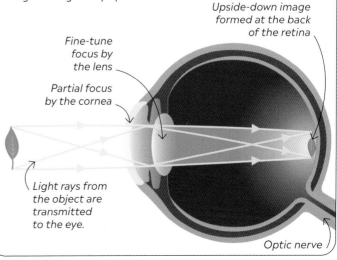

Upside-down image formed at the back of the retina

Fine-tune focus by the lens

Partial focus by the cornea

Light rays from the object are transmitted to the eye.

Optic nerve

Ears and hearing

After sight, hearing provides the brain with the most information about the outside world. It enables us to figure out the source, direction, and nature of sounds and to communicate with each other. Our ears detect waves of pressure, called sound waves, that travel through the air from a vibrating sound source. The ears turn these waves into nerve signals, which the brain interprets as sounds that range from loud to quiet and from high pitched to low.

Ear pioneer

The Examination of the Organ of Hearing, published in 1562 by the Italian anatomist Bartolomeo Eustachio, was probably the first major work devoted to ears.

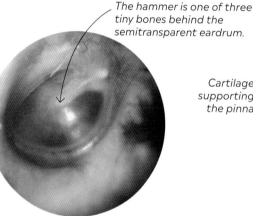

The hammer is one of three tiny bones behind the semitransparent eardrum.

The eardrum

The eardrum is a taut, delicate membrane, like the stretched skin on a drum, that vibrates when sound waves enter the ear. It separates the outer ear from the middle ear. Doctors can examine the eardrum through a medical instrument called an otoscope.

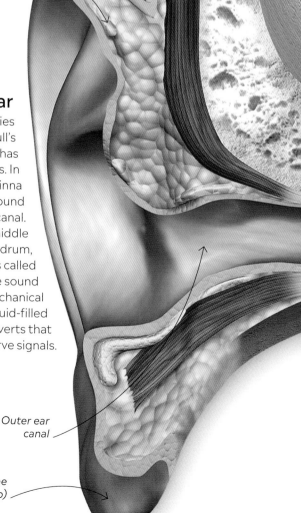

Temporal bone of the skull

Scalp muscle

Cartilage supporting the pinna

Outer ear canal

Ear lobe of the pinna (ear flap)

HEARING

Sound waves funneled into the ear canal strike the eardrum, making it vibrate. This makes the three ossicles move back and forth. The stirrup pushes and pulls the flexible oval window like a piston. This sets up vibrations in the fluid filling the cochlea. Inside the cochlea, sound-detecting hair cells turn the vibrations into nerve signals. These pass along the cochlear nerve to the hearing area of the brain.

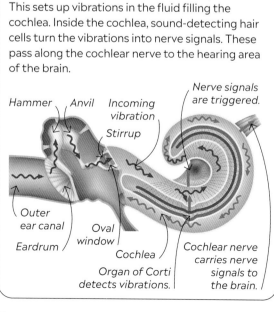

Hammer *Anvil* *Incoming vibration*

Nerve signals are triggered.

Stirrup

Outer ear canal

Oval window

Eardrum

Cochlea

Organ of Corti detects vibrations.

Cochlear nerve carries nerve signals to the brain.

Inside the ear

Most of the ear lies inside the skull's temporal bone. It has three main parts. In the outer ear, the pinna (ear flap) directs sound waves into the ear canal. In the air-filled middle ear, behind the eardrum, three tiny bones called ossicles convert the sound waves into mechanical movement. The fluid-filled inner ear converts that movement into nerve signals.

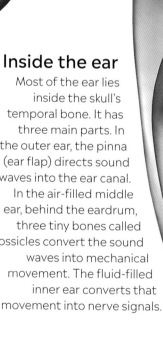

Inside the organ of Corti

When sound vibrations pass through the cochlea's fluid, hair cells (yellow) move up and down. This squashes them, causing hair cells to send signals to the brain. They do the same in the balance organs.

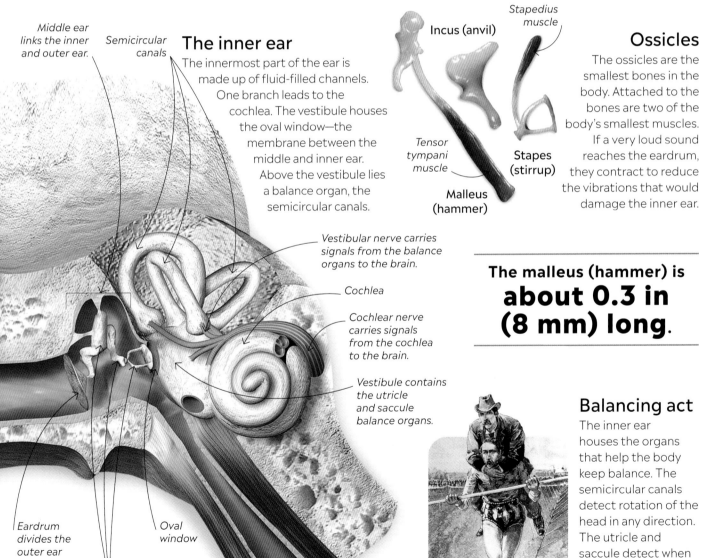

The inner ear

The innermost part of the ear is made up of fluid-filled channels. One branch leads to the cochlea. The vestibule houses the oval window—the membrane between the middle and inner ear. Above the vestibule lies a balance organ, the semicircular canals.

Middle ear links the inner and outer ear.

Semicircular canals

Incus (anvil)

Stapedius muscle

Tensor tympani muscle

Stapes (stirrup)

Malleus (hammer)

Vestibular nerve carries signals from the balance organs to the brain.

Cochlea

Cochlear nerve carries signals from the cochlea to the brain.

Vestibule contains the utricle and saccule balance organs.

Eardrum divides the outer ear from the middle ear.

Oval window

Ossicles (ear bones) link the eardrum to the oval window.

Eustachian tube

Ossicles

The ossicles are the smallest bones in the body. Attached to the bones are two of the body's smallest muscles. If a very loud sound reaches the eardrum, they contract to reduce the vibrations that would damage the inner ear.

The malleus (hammer) is about 0.3 in (8 mm) long.

Balancing act

The inner ear houses the organs that help the body keep balance. The semicircular canals detect rotation of the head in any direction. The utricle and saccule detect when the body accelerates. These balance organs constantly update the brain so that it can keep the body upright.

Smell and **taste**

The senses of smell and taste are closely linked—both detect chemicals. Taste receptors on the tongue detect substances in drink and food. Olfactory (smell) receptors in the nasal cavity pick up odor molecules in air. The two senses enable us to detect all kinds of scents and flavors, good and bad.

Cross-section inside the nose

The nasal cavity's lining (blue) contains thousands of smell receptor cells. The cells' hairlike cilia project into the watery mucus of the nasal lining. They detect odor molecules in the air and relay signals to the olfactory nerve, the olfactory bulb, and the brain.

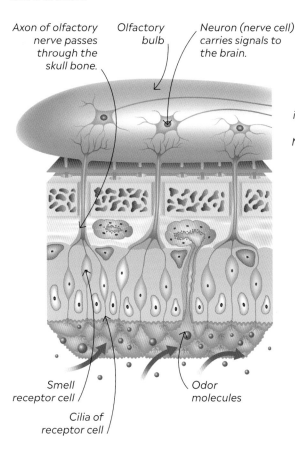

Axon of olfactory nerve passes through the skull bone.

Olfactory bulb

Neuron (nerve cell) carries signals to the brain.

Smell receptor cell

Cilia of receptor cell

Odor molecules

For centuries, physicians thought diseases were carried by foul-smelling air.

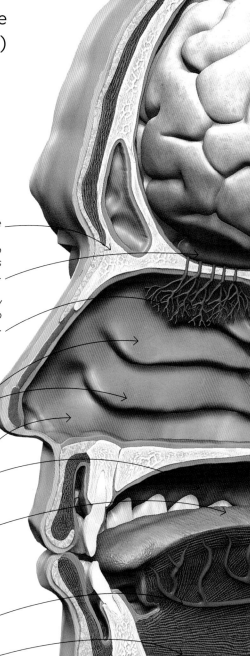

Skull bone

The olfactory bulb carries the smell signals to the front of the brain.

Branching olfactory nerves connect to the olfactory bulb.

Nasal conchae (shelves of bone covered in nasal lining) keep the air inside the nose moist.

Nasal cavity connects the nostrils to the throat

Mouth cavity

Tongue surface is covered with papillae, bearing taste buds.

The chorda tympani branch of the facial nerve carries taste signals from the front two-thirds of the tongue.

One of the muscles that move the tongue

Smell and taste

This cross-section shows the routes taken by nerve signals from smell receptors in the nose and from taste buds in the tongue. In the nasal cavity, the olfactory nerves send signals to the olfactory bulb, which carries the signals to the areas of the brain that identify smells. Taste signals from the tongue travel along separate nerves to the brain stem, then to the area of the brain where tastes are recognized.

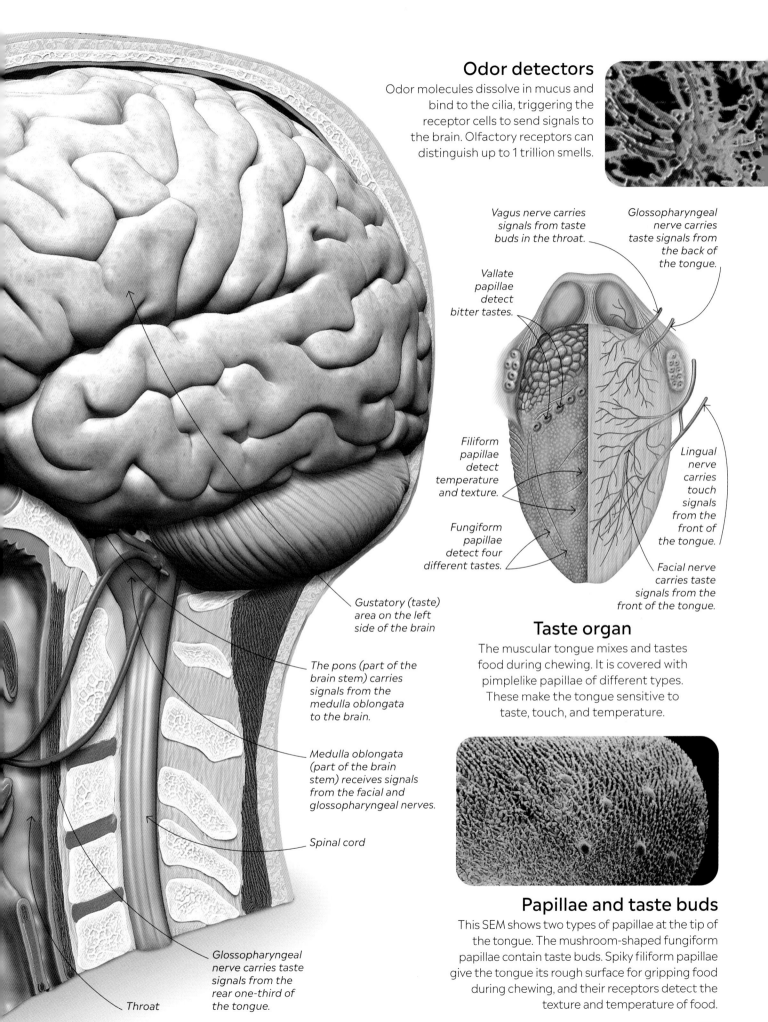

Odor detectors

Odor molecules dissolve in mucus and bind to the cilia, triggering the receptor cells to send signals to the brain. Olfactory receptors can distinguish up to 1 trillion smells.

Vagus nerve carries signals from taste buds in the throat.

Glossopharyngeal nerve carries taste signals from the back of the tongue.

Vallate papillae detect bitter tastes.

Filiform papillae detect temperature and texture.

Lingual nerve carries touch signals from the front of the tongue.

Fungiform papillae detect four different tastes.

Facial nerve carries taste signals from the front of the tongue.

Gustatory (taste) area on the left side of the brain

The pons (part of the brain stem) carries signals from the medulla oblongata to the brain.

Medulla oblongata (part of the brain stem) receives signals from the facial and glossopharyngeal nerves.

Spinal cord

Glossopharyngeal nerve carries taste signals from the rear one-third of the tongue.

Throat

Taste organ

The muscular tongue mixes and tastes food during chewing. It is covered with pimplelike papillae of different types. These make the tongue sensitive to taste, touch, and temperature.

Papillae and taste buds

This SEM shows two types of papillae at the tip of the tongue. The mushroom-shaped fungiform papillae contain taste buds. Spiky filiform papillae give the tongue its rough surface for gripping food during chewing, and their receptors detect the texture and temperature of food.

Hormones

A second control system works alongside the brain and nerve network. The endocrine system is a collection of glands that release chemical messengers, or hormones, into the bloodstream. They control body processes, such as growth and reproduction, by targeting specific body cells and altering their chemical activities. Located in the brain, the hypothalamus links the two control systems.

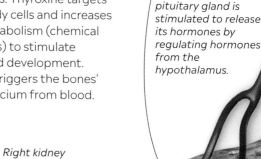

Hypothalamus

Nerve cells in the front of the hypothalamus produce the hormones oxytocin and ADH.

Pituitary stalk connects the hypothalamus to the pituitary gland.

Blood vessels carry regulating hormones from the hypothalamus to the front of the pituitary gland.

The front lobe of the pituitary gland is stimulated to release its hormones by regulating hormones from the hypothalamus.

Thyroid gland

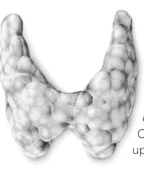

This gland makes two main hormones. Thyroxine targets most body cells and increases their metabolism (chemical processes) to stimulate growth and development. Calcitonin triggers the bones' uptake of calcium from blood.

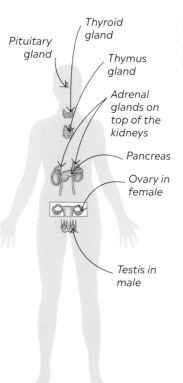

Pituitary gland
Thyroid gland
Thymus gland
Adrenal glands on top of the kidneys
Pancreas
Ovary in female
Testis in male

Adrenal glands

Right kidney

Adrenal gland

The outer parts of the two adrenal glands on the kidneys produce corticosteroids, hormones that regulate the levels of salt and water in the blood, speed up the body's metabolism, and deal with stress. The inside of each adrenal gland releases the hormone adrenaline.

Endocrine system

The glands that make up the endocrine system lie inside the head and torso. Some endocrine glands, such as the thyroid, are organs in their own right. Other glands are embedded in an organ that also has other functions.

The hormone adrenaline triggers our fight or flight response in the face of danger.

Hypothalamus

The almond-sized hypothalamus at the base of the brain controls many body activities. Nerve cells in the hypothalamus produce regulating hormones that travel to the front lobe of the pituitary to stimulate the release of pituitary hormones. The hypothalamus also makes two more hormones that nerve fibers carry to the rear of the pituitary.

Nerve cells in the rear of the hypothalamus release regulating hormones into the blood vessels supplying the front lobe.

Pancreas

Most of the tissues of the pancreas are gland cells that make digestive enzymes for release into the small intestine. The endocrine tissues release the hormones insulin and glucagon directly into the bloodstream. These two hormones maintain the steady levels of glucose—the sugar removed from food to fuel the body—in the blood.

Nerve fibers carry oxytocin and ADH to the rear lobe of the pituitary gland.

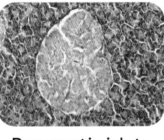

Pancreatic islets

The tissue inside the pancreas is dotted with more than one million clusters of cells called islets of Langerhans (center). In the 1890s, scientists discovered the cells released secretions, later called hormones.

Frederick Banting (1891-1941)

Charles Best (1899-1978)

The insulin story

A lack of the hormone insulin in the body causes a serious condition called diabetes, where blood glucose levels soar. In 1922, Canadian Frederick Banting and American Charles Best successfully extracted insulin so that it could be used to control this disorder.

Rear lobe of the pituitary gland stores and releases ADH and oxytocin.

Pituitary gland

The pea-sized pituitary gland is attached to the base of the brain. Cells in its front lobe (part) make six hormones that affect metabolism, growth, and reproduction. The rear lobe stores and releases antidiuretic hormone (ADH), which controls urine's water levels, and oxytocin, which makes the uterus contract during labor.

This electron microscope image shows undeveloped T cells (yellow) in the thymus gland.

Thymus gland

The thymus gland is large in childhood but shrinks in adult life. During the early years, it produces two hormones that ensure the development of white blood cells called T cells, or T lymphocytes. These identify and destroy disease-causing organisms.

The heart

Organ storage
In Egyptian mummies, most body organs were removed and stored in jars such as these. The heart was left in place, ready for the afterlife.

The ancient Egyptians believed the heart housed the soul, whereas the ancient Greeks thought it was the seat of love. In fact, it is an extraordinarily reliable, muscular pump, with a right and left side. Each side has two linked chambers—an upper, thin-walled atrium and a larger, thick-walled ventricle below. The right ventricle pumps oxygen-poor blood to the lungs to pick up oxygen and then back to the left atrium. The left ventricle pumps oxygen-rich blood around the body and back to the right atrium.

Coronary sinus (main coronary vein)

Right coronary artery

Aorta

Left coronary artery

Coronary circulation
The heart's wall has its own blood supply called the coronary circulation, which delivers oxygen to keep the heart beating. Left and right coronary arteries stem from the aorta and branch out to carry oxygen-rich blood to all parts of the heart wall. Oxygen-poor blood is taken by coronary veins to the coronary sinus. This vein at the back of the heart empties blood into the right atrium, ready to go around the heart again.

Small connecting blood vessels

Coronary vein

Main branch of the left coronary artery

Valve open

Valve closed

Blood flows away from the heart.

Blood pushes through the open valve as the heart contracts.

Blood flows back and shuts the valve as the heart relaxes.

Blood is pumped out of the heart.

Valves at work
Valves ensure the one-way flow of blood. The aortic and pulmonary valves at the two exits from the heart have flaps of tissue. When the heart contracts, blood flows out, pressing the flaps open. When the heart relaxes, blood tries to flow back, pressing the flaps shut.

Heart rate
The average adult heart beats 60–80 times, pumping up to 11 pints (6 liters) of blood, every minute. Each beat creates a pressure surge through the body's arteries. During activity, the muscles need more oxygen and nutrients, so the heart beats faster and harder.

 **EYEWITNESS**

Helen Brooke Taussig
U.S. physician Helen B. Taussig (1898–1986), the founder of pediatric cardiology, helped develop a treatment for a condition called "blue baby syndrome." After she became deaf in her 30s, she came up with an innovative method of assessing a patient's heartbeat by using her hands.

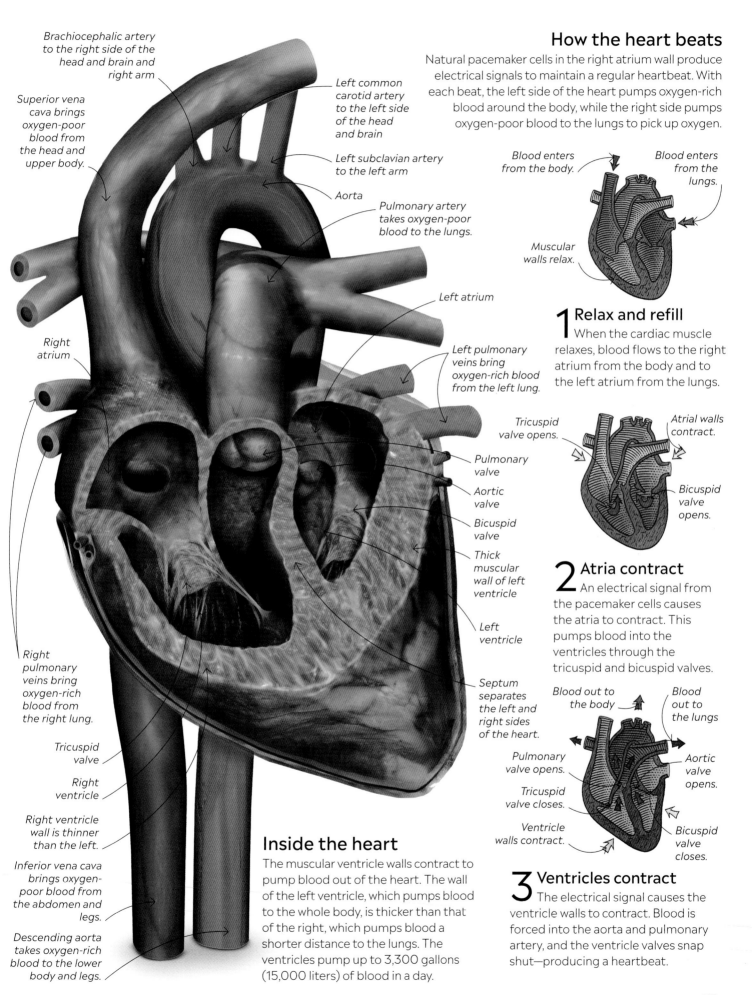

Brachiocephalic artery to the right side of the head and brain and right arm

Superior vena cava brings oxygen-poor blood from the head and upper body.

Left common carotid artery to the left side of the head and brain

Left subclavian artery to the left arm

Aorta

Pulmonary artery takes oxygen-poor blood to the lungs.

Right atrium

Left atrium

Left pulmonary veins bring oxygen-rich blood from the left lung.

Pulmonary valve

Aortic valve

Bicuspid valve

Thick muscular wall of left ventricle

Left ventricle

Right pulmonary veins bring oxygen-rich blood from the right lung.

Septum separates the left and right sides of the heart.

Tricuspid valve

Right ventricle

Right ventricle wall is thinner than the left.

Inferior vena cava brings oxygen-poor blood from the abdomen and legs.

Descending aorta takes oxygen-rich blood to the lower body and legs.

Inside the heart

The muscular ventricle walls contract to pump blood out of the heart. The wall of the left ventricle, which pumps blood to the whole body, is thicker than that of the right, which pumps blood a shorter distance to the lungs. The ventricles pump up to 3,300 gallons (15,000 liters) of blood in a day.

How the heart beats

Natural pacemaker cells in the right atrium wall produce electrical signals to maintain a regular heartbeat. With each beat, the left side of the heart pumps oxygen-rich blood around the body, while the right side pumps oxygen-poor blood to the lungs to pick up oxygen.

Blood enters from the body.

Blood enters from the lungs.

Muscular walls relax.

1 Relax and refill
When the cardiac muscle relaxes, blood flows to the right atrium from the body and to the left atrium from the lungs.

Tricuspid valve opens.

Atrial walls contract.

Bicuspid valve opens.

2 Atria contract
An electrical signal from the pacemaker cells causes the atria to contract. This pumps blood into the ventricles through the tricuspid and bicuspid valves.

Blood out to the body

Blood out to the lungs

Pulmonary valve opens.

Aortic valve opens.

Tricuspid valve closes.

Ventricle walls contract.

Bicuspid valve closes.

3 Ventricles contract
The electrical signal causes the ventricle walls to contract. Blood is forced into the aorta and pulmonary artery, and the ventricle valves snap shut—producing a heartbeat.

In circulation

The body's trillions of cells need a constant supply of oxygen, nutrients, and other essentials and the constant removal of wastes. The heart pumps blood around the body, delivering essentials to cells through a vast network of blood vessels. A second transport system, called the lymphatic system, drains excess fluid from the tissues. The two systems also play key roles in fighting disease.

CIRCULATORY SYSTEM

Arteries carry oxygen-rich blood from the heart to body tissues, and veins return oxygen-poor blood from the tissues to the heart. Capillaries, too small to be seen here, carry blood through the tissues and connect arteries to veins.

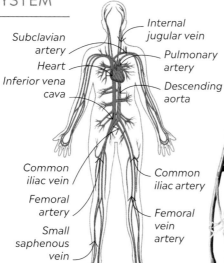

- Subclavian artery
- Internal jugular vein
- Pulmonary artery
- Heart
- Inferior vena cava
- Descending aorta
- Common iliac vein
- Common iliac artery
- Femoral artery
- Femoral vein artery
- Small saphenous vein

 EYEWITNESS

Ibn al-Nafis

Arab physician Ibn al-Nafis (1213–1288) is known for his groundbreaking insights into the body's circulatory system. He was the first person to describe the movement of blood from the right side of the heart through the lungs to the heart's left side.

- External iliac artery
- External iliac vein
- Pelvis (hip bone)
- Femoral vein carries blood from the thigh.

Blood vessels of the leg

The external iliac artery carries oxygen-rich blood from the heart to the leg. Here, it divides into branches that then subdivide to form the microscopic capillaries that deliver oxygen and nutrients to cells and remove their waste products. The capillaries then rejoin, forming larger vessels that connect into the network of major veins that carry oxygen-poor blood from the leg back toward the heart.

Branch of femoral artery supplies blood to the thigh.

William Harvey

Round and round

Until the 17th century, blood was thought to flow backward and forward inside arteries and veins. English physician William Harvey (1578–1657) showed how the heart pumped blood around the body in one direction.

The small saphenous vein carries blood from the foot and lower leg.

Small posterior tibial arteries supply blood to the foot and lower leg.

BLOOD VESSELS

With every heartbeat, an artery's walls expand and shrink as blood from the heart surges through it at high pressure. Veins carry blood returning from capillaries at low pressure, so their wall layers are thinner and less muscular. Just one cell thick, capillary walls let food and oxygen pass from blood into the surrounding tissues.

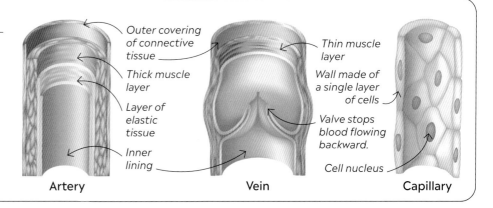

Outer covering of connective tissue

Thick muscle layer

Layer of elastic tissue

Inner lining

Thin muscle layer

Wall made of a single layer of cells

Valve stops blood flowing backward.

Cell nucleus

Artery

Vein

Capillary

Fighting infection

Every day, the body is exposed to pathogens—microscopic organisms, such as bacteria and viruses, that cause disease if they invade the body's tissues and bloodstream. White blood cells in the circulatory and lymphatic systems form part of the body's immune, or defense, system. Some patrol the body and search for invaders to destroy. Others attack specific pathogens and retain a memory of them, in case the same pathogens return.

Immune system

The macrophages and lymphocytes—white blood cells also called T and B cells—of the immune system respond to the invasion of pathogens by detecting and destroying them.

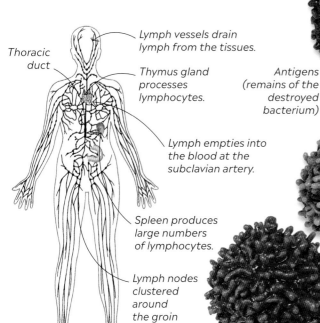

Thoracic duct

Lymph vessels drain lymph from the tissues.

Thymus gland processes lymphocytes.

Antigens (remains of the destroyed bacterium)

Lymph empties into the blood at the subclavian artery.

Spleen produces large numbers of lymphocytes.

Lymph nodes clustered around the groin

Helper T cell

Plasma cell

B cell

Macrophage

Shigella bacterium

Antibody

Antibodies attach themselves to the bacterium.

1 Capturing a pathogen

Macrophages are white blood cells that hunt for pathogens in the body's tissues. This one has captured a bacterium called *Shigella* and will eat it up.

2 Recognizing antigens

The macrophage displays antigens, or the remains of the bacterium, on its surface to activate a helper T cell.

Lymphatic system

This network of vessels drains excess fluid from the body's tissues and returns it to the bloodstream. The contractions of skeletal muscles push the fluid (lymph) along the lymph vessels, and as it flows, lymph passes through small swellings called lymph nodes.

3 Spurred into action

The helper T cell releases substances that switch on a B cell that targets *Shigella*. The B cell multiplies to produce plasma cells.

4 Making antibodies

Plasma cells release billions of antibody molecules into the blood and lymph. The antibodies can then attach to any *Shigella* bacteria present in the body.

5 Disabling the pathogen

Antibodies bind to the antigens on the *Shigella* bacterium's surface. This tags it for macrophages or other white blood cells to destroy.

The blood

An average adult has 9 pints (5 liters) of blood coursing around the body. Each drop of blood consists of millions of cells floating in liquid plasma. Red blood cells deliver essential oxygen to the body's tissues, while defense cells fight off infections. Blood also distributes heat to keep the body at a steady 98.6°F (37°C)—the ideal temperature for cells to function.

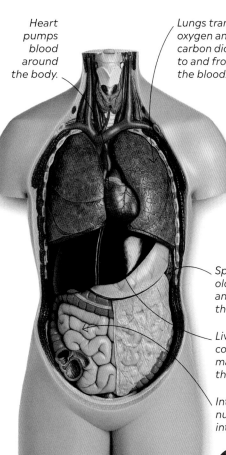

Heart pumps blood around the body.

Lungs transfer oxygen and carbon dioxide to and from the blood.

Spleen removes old red blood cells and helps recycle their iron.

Liver controls the concentration of many chemicals in the blood.

Intestines transfer nutrients from food into the blood.

Three main roles

Blood transports a range of substances, including oxygen, nutrients, and waste products from cells. It also protects the body by carrying white blood cells and forming blood clots. And it controls body temperature by distributing heat produced by organs around the body.

Blood transfusions

Before the discovery of blood groups, the transfusion (transfer) of blood from a donor—usually a healthy person, but here a dog—to a sick patient, often failed, killing the patient.

Blood groups

Austrian-American scientist Karl Landsteiner (1868–1943) found that people belonged to one of four blood groups: A, B, AB, or O. Doctors can now match up blood types to keep a body from rejecting a blood transfusion from the wrong blood group.

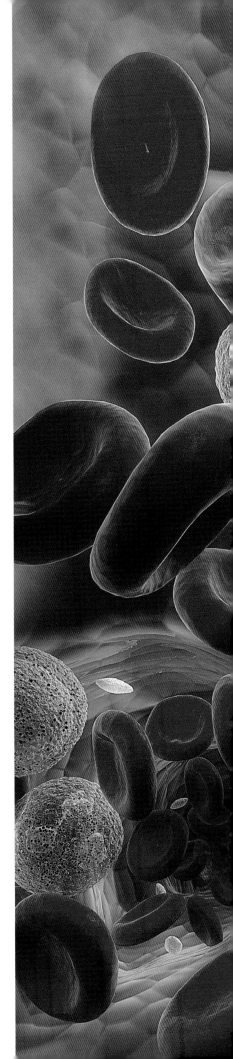

Blood components

If allowed to settle, blood separates into three parts. The red and white blood cells float in a yellow liquid called plasma. This is mainly water containing more than 100 substances, including blood proteins.

Plasma makes up 55% of blood.

White blood cells and platelets make up 1% of blood.

Red blood cells make up 44% of blood.

Settled blood

Changing color

Blood takes its color from the red blood cells. When they pick up oxygen in the lungs, blood turns bright red. Once they unload oxygen in the tissues, blood turns a darker shade. of red.

Oxygen-rich blood　　**Oxygen-poor blood**

Oxygen carrier

The protein hemoglobin carries oxygen. A molecule of hemoglobin contains four iron atoms (yellow), which bind oxygen in the lungs and release it wherever oxygen is in short supply in the body.

FORMING BLOOD CLOTS

When there is a wound, platelets stick together to briefly form a plug. They also release chemicals that convert a blood protein into threads of fibrin, which trap blood cells to form a clot. White blood cells destroy any invading bacteria. The clot dries out to form a protective scab over the tissues while they repair themselves.

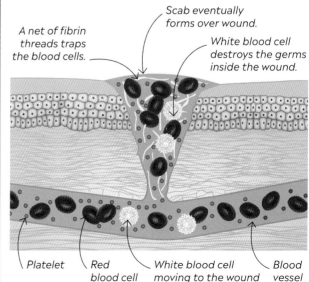

A net of fibrin threads traps the blood cells.

Scab eventually forms over wound.

White blood cell destroys the germs inside the wound.

Platelet　Red blood cell　White blood cell moving to the wound　Blood vessel

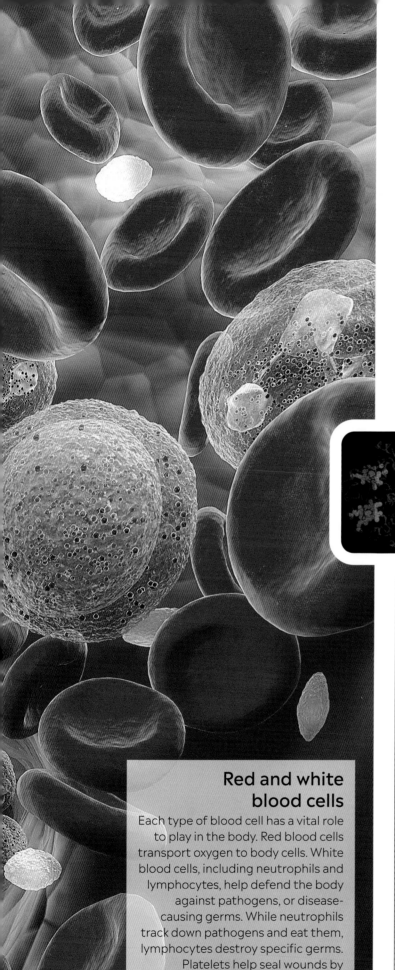

Red and white blood cells

Each type of blood cell has a vital role to play in the body. Red blood cells transport oxygen to body cells. White blood cells, including neutrophils and lymphocytes, help defend the body against pathogens, or disease-causing germs. While neutrophils track down pathogens and eat them, lymphocytes destroy specific germs. Platelets help seal wounds by forming blood clots.

Breathing
to live

The body can survive without food or water for some time, but it soon dies if breathing stops. Breathing brings fresh air containing oxygen into the lungs and then expels stale air containing waste carbon dioxide.

The nasal cavity (space) connects the nostrils to the throat.

Three conchae (shelves of bone covered in nasal lining) keep the air inside the nose moist.

The nostril contains nose hairs to filter out dirt.

Mouth cavity

Tongue

Epiglottis

Vocal cords

Larynx (voice box)

Esophagus

Trachea (windpipe)

Nasal cavity

Trachea (windpipe)

Right lung

Intercostal muscles between the ribs

Rib

Respiratory system

The respiratory system carries air into the body through its airways—the nasal cavity, throat, larynx, trachea, and its branches—to a pair of lungs. The lungs are protected by the ribs.

Controlled breathing

Musicians such as Charlie Parker (left) and Miles Davis need great breath control to play wind instruments. Precisely timed contractions of the diaphragm and rib muscles push bursts of air out of the mouth and into the instrument.

Upper airways

The lungs' delicate tissues are easily damaged by dirt particles, which must be removed in the upper airways after inhalation (breathing in). Nostril hairs filter out larger dirt particles. Sticky mucus covering the nasal lining traps dust and bacteria. The filtered air then passes into the larynx and on to the lungs.

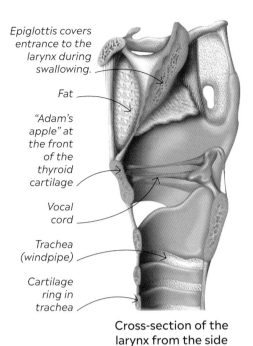

Epiglottis covers entrance to the larynx during swallowing.

Fat

"Adam's apple" at the front of the thyroid cartilage

Vocal cord

Trachea (windpipe)

Cartilage ring in trachea

Cross-section of the larynx from the side

Larynx

During breathing, air passes from the throat, through the larynx, to the trachea (windpipe). The larynx, also called the voice box, is made of nine pieces of cartilage. During swallowing, the entrance to the larynx is covered by a flap of cartilage, called the epiglottis, to prevent food from entering the trachea. The vocal cords are two membrane-covered ligaments that produce sound (see below).

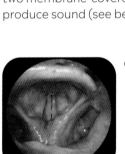

Closed

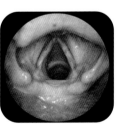

Open

Vocal cords

Inside the throat, when the vocal cords are relaxed, they open to let air in and out for breathing. To make sounds, they are pulled taut as controlled bursts of air are pushed out, making the closed vocal cords vibrate. The tongue and lips turn sounds into speech.

BREATHING IN AND OUT

Air is sucked in down the trachea.

Intercostal muscles pull ribs.

Lung swells.

Ribs move upward and also outward.

Air is blown out.

Lung shrinks.

Ribs move inward and downward.

Diaphragm contracts and flattens out.

Diaphragm relaxes back into a dome shape.

Inhalation
For inhalation (breathing in), the diaphragm and intercostal muscles contract to expand the space inside the chest. As the lungs swell to fill the expanded chest, air is sucked in.

Exhalation
For exhalation (breathing out), the diaphragm and intercostal muscles relax. The rib cage falls, and the diaphragm is pushed up by the organs below it. This squeezes the lungs, and air is forced back outside.

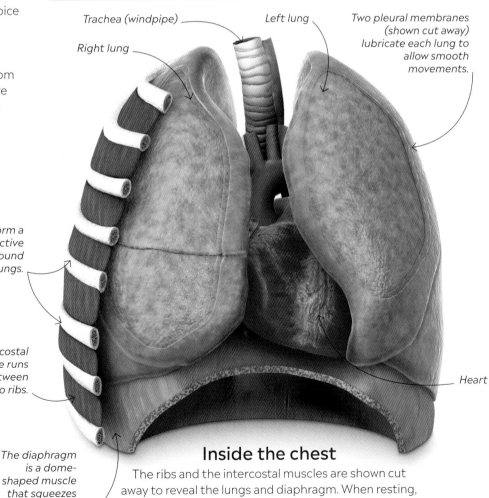

Trachea (windpipe)

Right lung

Left lung

Two pleural membranes (shown cut away) lubricate each lung to allow smooth movements.

Ribs form a protective cage around the lungs.

Intercostal muscle runs between two ribs.

The diaphragm is a dome-shaped muscle that squeezes the lungs when we breathe out.

Heart

Inside the chest

The ribs and the intercostal muscles are shown cut away to reveal the lungs and diaphragm. When resting, the body breathes at a rate of around 15 times a minute. During exercise, the need for oxygen increases, and so the rate rises up to 50 times a minute.

Inside the lungs

The lungs are filled with millions of microscopic air sacs called alveoli, each wrapped in a mesh of tiny blood vessels. Alveoli take oxygen from the air we breathe in and pass it into the bloodstream, which delivers oxygen to every body cell to release energy from food in a process known as cell respiration. In exchange, the waste product, carbon dioxide, travels in the bloodstream to the alveoli, where it is expelled.

All-over respiration

Italian scientist Lazzaro Spallanzani (1729–1799) proposed that respiration took place not just in the lungs but in every cell of the body. He also discovered that blood delivers oxygen to body tissues and carries away carbon dioxide.

Oxygen gets its name

French chemist Antoine Lavoisier (1743–1794) showed that a candle burned using part of the air (a gas he called oxygen) and produced a waste gas (now called carbon dioxide). He suggested that animals live by burning food inside the lungs with the oxygen in air—a process he called respiration.

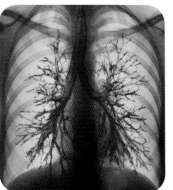

X-ray of the bronchial tree

A branching system of tubes carries air all through the lungs. The trachea divides into two bronchi, one to each lung. Each bronchus splits into many smaller bronchi, then bronchioles, and finally terminal bronchioles, narrower than a hair.

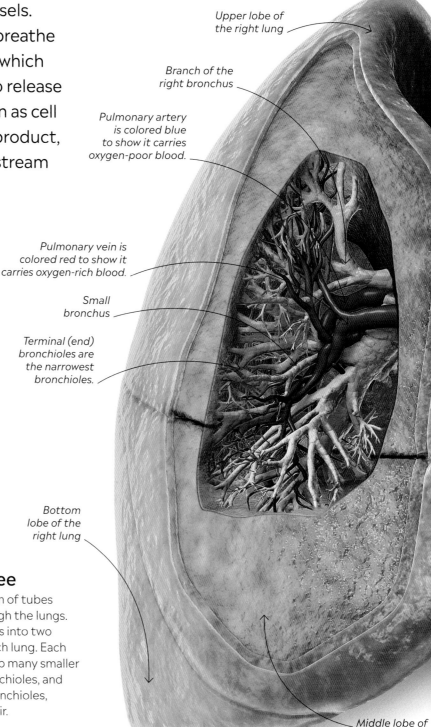

Upper lobe of the right lung

Branch of the right bronchus

Pulmonary artery is colored blue to show it carries oxygen-poor blood.

Pulmonary vein is colored red to show it carries oxygen-rich blood.

Small bronchus

Terminal (end) bronchioles are the narrowest bronchioles.

Bottom lobe of the right lung

Middle lobe of the right lung

Micro-bubbles

This SEM shows red blood cells in an artery in lung tissue. Around the artery are bubble-like alveoli, measuring less than 0.004 in (0.1 mm) across.

Where gas exchange happens

The lungs' 300 million alveoli provide a combined surface area for gas exchange the size of a tennis court. Around each alveolus is a network of blood capillaries that exchange gases with the alveolus.

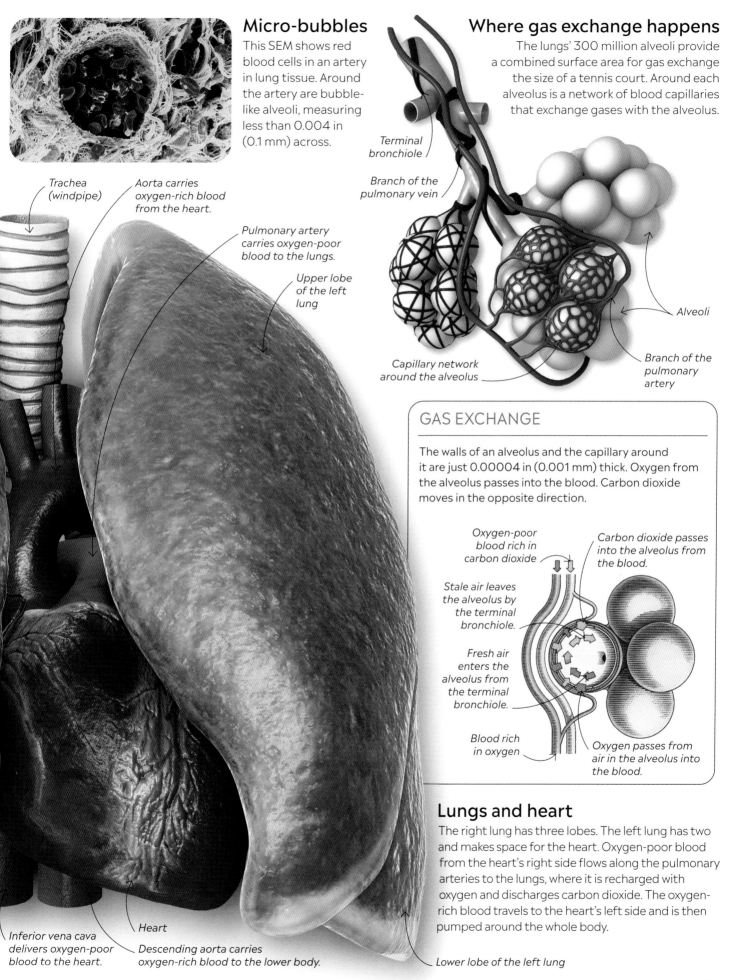

Trachea (windpipe)

Aorta carries oxygen-rich blood from the heart.

Pulmonary artery carries oxygen-poor blood to the lungs.

Upper lobe of the left lung

Terminal bronchiole

Branch of the pulmonary vein

Alveoli

Capillary network around the alveolus

Branch of the pulmonary artery

GAS EXCHANGE

The walls of an alveolus and the capillary around it are just 0.00004 in (0.001 mm) thick. Oxygen from the alveolus passes into the blood. Carbon dioxide moves in the opposite direction.

Oxygen-poor blood rich in carbon dioxide

Carbon dioxide passes into the alveolus from the blood.

Stale air leaves the alveolus by the terminal bronchiole.

Fresh air enters the alveolus from the terminal bronchiole.

Blood rich in oxygen

Oxygen passes from air in the alveolus into the blood.

Inferior vena cava delivers oxygen-poor blood to the heart.

Heart

Descending aorta carries oxygen-rich blood to the lower body.

Lower lobe of the left lung

Lungs and heart

The right lung has three lobes. The left lung has two and makes space for the heart. Oxygen-poor blood from the heart's right side flows along the pulmonary arteries to the lungs, where it is recharged with oxygen and discharges carbon dioxide. The oxygen-rich blood travels to the heart's left side and is then pumped around the whole body.

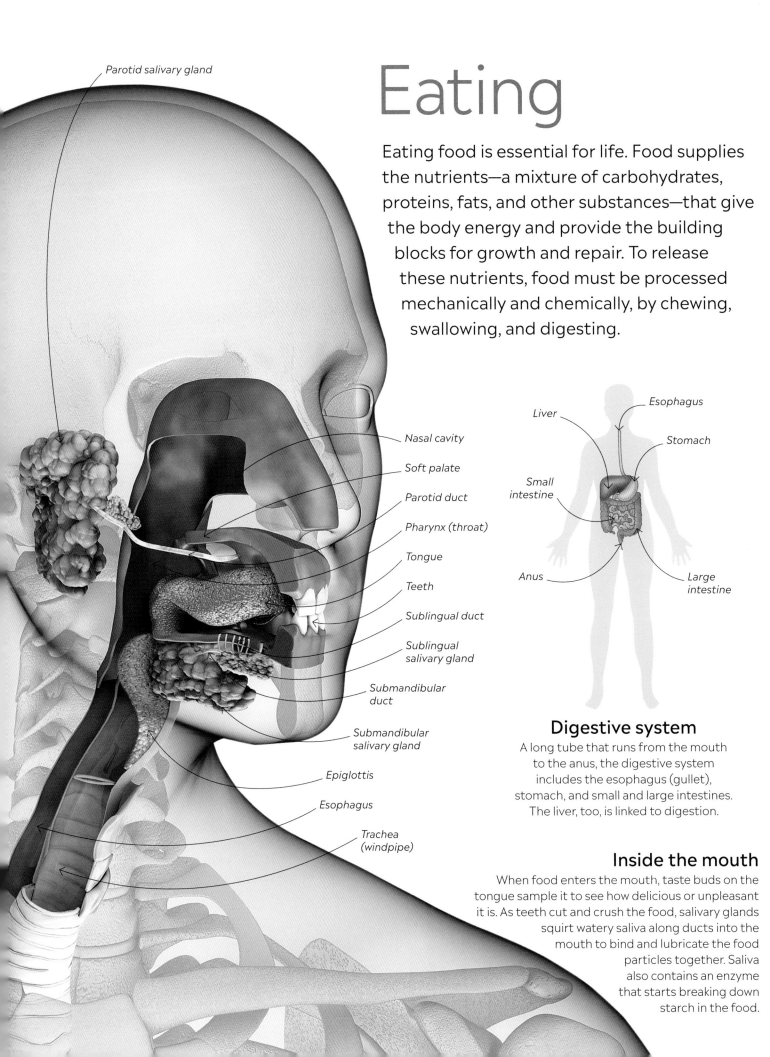

Eating

Eating food is essential for life. Food supplies the nutrients—a mixture of carbohydrates, proteins, fats, and other substances—that give the body energy and provide the building blocks for growth and repair. To release these nutrients, food must be processed mechanically and chemically, by chewing, swallowing, and digesting.

Parotid salivary gland

Nasal cavity

Soft palate

Parotid duct

Pharynx (throat)

Tongue

Teeth

Sublingual duct

Sublingual salivary gland

Submandibular duct

Submandibular salivary gland

Epiglottis

Esophagus

Trachea (windpipe)

Liver

Esophagus

Stomach

Small intestine

Anus

Large intestine

Digestive system
A long tube that runs from the mouth to the anus, the digestive system includes the esophagus (gullet), stomach, and small and large intestines. The liver, too, is linked to digestion.

Inside the mouth
When food enters the mouth, taste buds on the tongue sample it to see how delicious or unpleasant it is. As teeth cut and crush the food, salivary glands squirt watery saliva along ducts into the mouth to bind and lubricate the food particles together. Saliva also contains an enzyme that starts breaking down starch in the food.

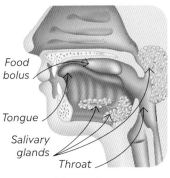
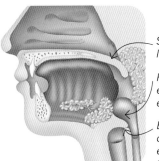
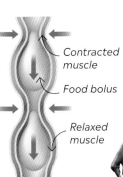
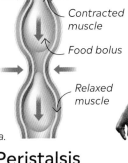

Food bolus

Tongue

Salivary glands

Throat

Soft palate lifted up

Food bolus enters the esophagus.

Epiglottis covers the entrance to the trachea.

Contracted muscle

Food bolus

Relaxed muscle

Chewing

As we chew, our teeth cut and crush food into small particles. Our tongue mixes the food with the mucus in saliva to form a slippery bolus, or ball of food, and pushes it into the throat.

Swallowing

The tongue pushing back triggers the throat muscles to contract, moving the bolus into the esophagus. The soft palate and epiglottis keep food from entering the nasal cavity and trachea.

Peristalsis

Peristalsis, or waves of muscle contractions, squeezes the bolus down the esophagus to the stomach and also through the intestines.

A balanced diet

A well-balanced diet provides important nutrients to our body. Grains contain carbohydrates (starches and sugars) for energy. Fish and meat contain proteins that build and maintain the body, plus a little fat, for energy. Vegetables (and fruit) have vitamins and minerals that help cells work well, and fiber helps the intestines work better. Dairy products provide calcium to our body.

Energy release

Running, like any physical activity, requires the energy that comes from food. Digestion converts food starches into sugars and fats into fatty acids. Broken down inside muscle cells, these fuels release energy for movement.

Teeth

Our teeth break up food to make it easier to swallow and digest. During childhood, baby teeth are replaced by a set of adult, permanent teeth. These include chisel-like incisors that cut and slice at the front, pointed canines that grip and tear, and flat premolars and molars that crush and grind at the back.

Adult tooth will push out baby tooth as it grows.

Five-year teeth
The first 20 baby teeth appear from the age of six months. From about the age of six, they begin to fall out.

Full set of adult teeth
By early adulthood, all 32 adult teeth have come through. Each half jaw has two incisors, one canine, two premolars, and three molars.

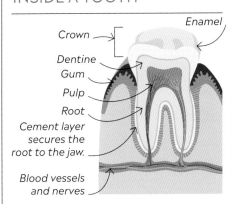

Upper third molar (wisdom tooth) may or may not appear.

Root anchors tooth in jawbone.

INSIDE A TOOTH

Crown

Enamel

Dentine

Gum

Pulp

Root

Cement layer secures the root to the jaw.

Blood vessels and nerves

Bonelike dentine forms the tooth's root and supports a rock-hard crown of nonliving enamel for grinding up food. The central cavity contains living pulp tissue fed by blood vessels and by nerve endings that sense pressure as we bite and chew.

Digestion

After being swallowed, it takes about 10 seconds for chewed food to reach the stomach, where digestion takes place. The stomach starts to break down food with enzymes (chemical digesters) and churns it into liquid chyme, which it releases into the small intestine. Here, further enzymes digest food into its simplest components. These nutrients are then absorbed into the bloodstream and circulated to the body's cells.

Gastric pits

Millions of gastric pits dot the stomach's lining. Through these tiny holes, gastric glands release gastric juice into the stomach. The juice produces an enzyme that digests the proteins in food. Mucus in the juice coats the stomach lining and prevents the juice from digesting the lining itself.

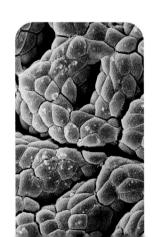

The body's chemical factory

Our largest internal organ, the liver helps balance the chemical makeup of blood. As oxygen-rich blood from the heart and nutrient-rich blood from the intestines pass through the liver, it releases nutrients into the bloodstream or stores them for future use. It also makes bile, removes poisons from the blood, destroys bacteria, and recycles worn-out red blood cells.

Food-processor

The stomach is a J-shaped bag that expands as it receives food through the esophagus (gullet) and processes it for the next few hours. Its muscular wall contracts to churn up the food, while acidic gastric (stomach) juice digests the food's proteins. The end result is a soupy liquid called chyme. This is released slowly into the small intestine.

The intestines

The small intestine is about 20 ft (6 m) long and has three sections. The short duodenum receives chyme from the stomach and digestive fluids from the liver and pancreas. In the jejunum and ileum, digestion is completed, and nutrients are absorbed. The large intestine is just 5 ft (1.5 m) long. Here, watery waste from the ileum dries out and forms feces to store in the rectum.

Esophagus

Left lobe of the liver

Stomach has a muscular wall.

The transverse colon conceals the duodenum connecting the stomach to the jejunum.

Jejunum is the middle section of the small intestine.

Descending colon

Right lobe of the liver

Gallbladder stores bile.

Ascending colon

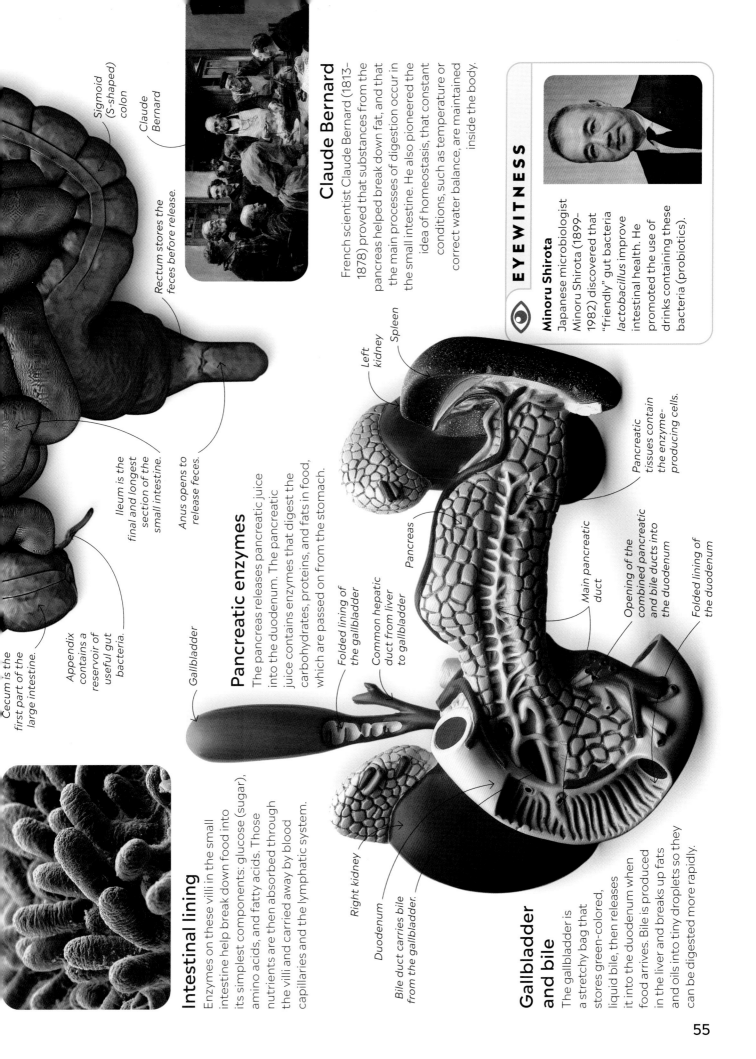

Sigmoid (S-shaped) colon

Claude Bernard

Rectum stores the feces before release.

Claude Bernard

French scientist Claude Bernard (1813–1878) proved that substances from the pancreas helped break down fat, and that the main processes of digestion occur in the small intestine. He also pioneered the idea of homeostasis, that constant conditions, such as temperature or correct water balance, are maintained inside the body.

EYEWITNESS

Minoru Shirota
Japanese microbiologist Minoru Shirota (1899–1982) discovered that "friendly" gut bacteria *lactobacillus* improve intestinal health. He promoted the use of drinks containing these bacteria (probiotics).

Ileum is the final and longest section of the small intestine.

Anus opens to release feces.

Cecum is the first part of the large intestine.

Appendix contains a reservoir of useful gut bacteria.

Gallbladder

Left kidney

Spleen

Pancreatic tissues contain the enzyme-producing cells.

Folded lining of the gallbladder

Common hepatic duct from liver to gallbladder

Pancreas

Main pancreatic duct

Opening of the combined pancreatic and bile ducts into the duodenum

Folded lining of the duodenum

Right kidney

Duodenum

Bile duct carries bile from the gallbladder.

Intestinal lining

Enzymes on these villi in the small intestine help break down food into its simplest components: glucose (sugar), amino acids, and fatty acids. Those nutrients are then absorbed through the villi and carried away by blood capillaries and the lymphatic system.

Pancreatic enzymes

The pancreas releases pancreatic juice into the duodenum. The pancreatic juice contains enzymes that digest the carbohydrates, proteins, and fats in food, which are passed on from the stomach.

Gallbladder and bile

The gallbladder is a stretchy bag that stores green-colored, liquid bile, then releases it into the duodenum when food arrives. Bile is produced in the liver and breaks up fats and oils into tiny droplets so they can be digested more rapidly.

Waste disposal

Bladder control

When a baby's bladder is full of urine, the stretch receptors in its muscular wall automatically tell it to empty. Young children learn to control this reflex action.

Body cells continually release waste substances into the bloodstream. If left to build up, they would poison the body. The urinary system disposes of waste by cleansing the blood as it passes through a pair of kidneys. It also removes excess water to ensure that the body's water content stays the same.

Aristotle

The Greek philosopher Aristotle (384–322 BCE) challenged ideas about anatomy by looking inside the real bodies of animals and humans and recording what he saw. He provided the first descriptions of the urinary system and how it works.

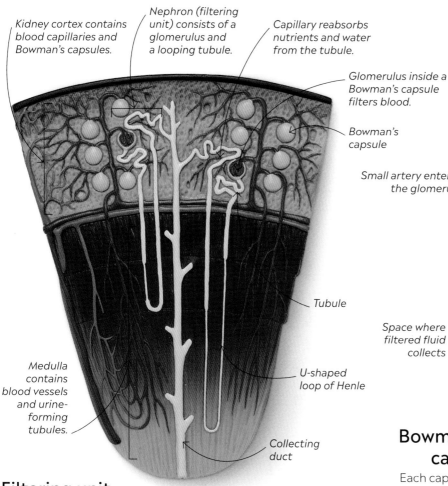

Kidney cortex contains blood capillaries and Bowman's capsules.

Nephron (filtering unit) consists of a glomerulus and a looping tubule.

Capillary reabsorbs nutrients and water from the tubule.

Glomerulus inside a Bowman's capsule filters blood.

Bowman's capsule

Tubule

Medulla contains blood vessels and urine-forming tubules.

U-shaped loop of Henle

Collecting duct

Small artery leaving the glomerulus

Small artery entering the glomerulus

Space where filtered fluid collects

Capillary of the glomerulus

Start of tubule

Filtering unit

Each kidney's blood-filtering unit, or nephron, links to a long tubule. This loops from the cortex to the medulla and back, then joins a collecting duct. As fluid filtered from blood passes along the nephron, useful substances are absorbed back into the bloodstream, leaving waste urine to flow into the collecting duct.

Bowman's capsule

Each capsule surrounds a glomerulus, or cluster of capillaries. They filter the blood and produce a fluid. It contains not only waste but also such substances as glucose (sugar), which are useful to the body.

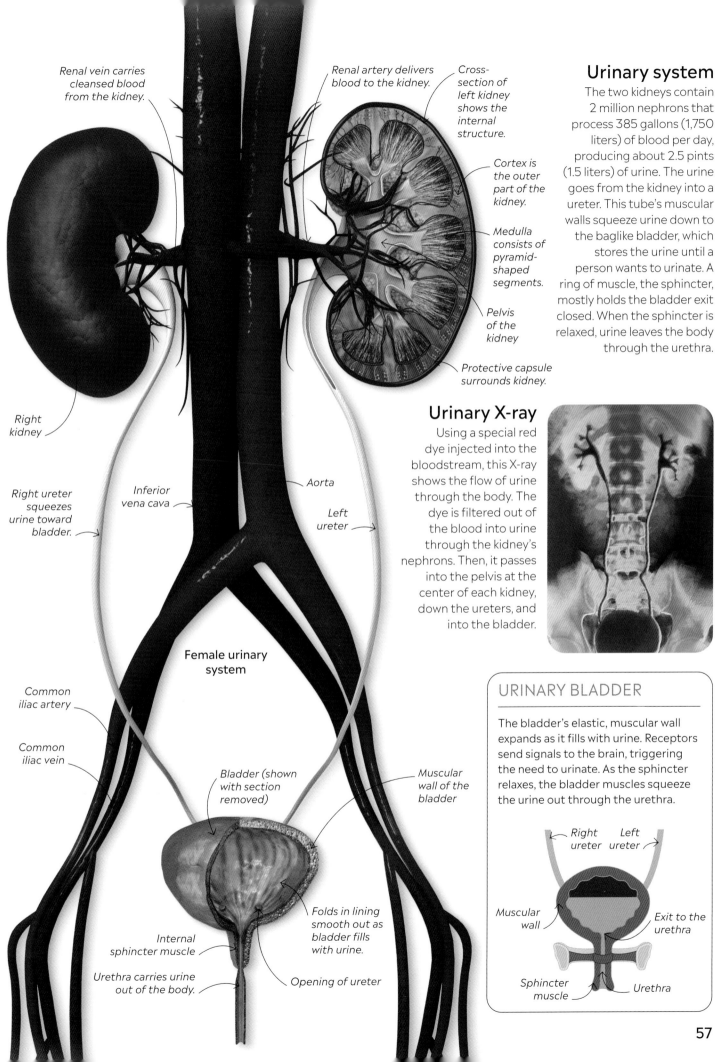

Renal vein carries cleansed blood from the kidney.

Renal artery delivers blood to the kidney.

Cross-section of left kidney shows the internal structure.

Urinary system

The two kidneys contain 2 million nephrons that process 385 gallons (1,750 liters) of blood per day, producing about 2.5 pints (1.5 liters) of urine. The urine goes from the kidney into a ureter. This tube's muscular walls squeeze urine down to the baglike bladder, which stores the urine until a person wants to urinate. A ring of muscle, the sphincter, mostly holds the bladder exit closed. When the sphincter is relaxed, urine leaves the body through the urethra.

Cortex is the outer part of the kidney.

Medulla consists of pyramid-shaped segments.

Pelvis of the kidney

Protective capsule surrounds kidney.

Right kidney

Right ureter squeezes urine toward bladder.

Inferior vena cava

Aorta

Left ureter

Urinary X-ray

Using a special red dye injected into the bloodstream, this X-ray shows the flow of urine through the body. The dye is filtered out of the blood into urine through the kidney's nephrons. Then, it passes into the pelvis at the center of each kidney, down the ureters, and into the bladder.

Female urinary system

Common iliac artery

Common iliac vein

Bladder (shown with section removed)

Muscular wall of the bladder

URINARY BLADDER

The bladder's elastic, muscular wall expands as it fills with urine. Receptors send signals to the brain, triggering the need to urinate. As the sphincter relaxes, the bladder muscles squeeze the urine out through the urethra.

Right ureter

Left ureter

Muscular wall

Exit to the urethra

Sphincter muscle

Urethra

Internal sphincter muscle

Folds in lining smooth out as bladder fills with urine.

Urethra carries urine out of the body.

Opening of ureter

Reproductive systems

Humans reproduce to pass on their genes and continue the cycle of life. Most human bodies have one of two reproductive systems. These reproductive systems are usually called male and female. Sexual intercourse (sex) between two people with different reproductive systems brings eggs and sperm together. These sex cells contain half of each partner's DNA (genetic instructions), which combine during fertilization to create a new life.

Regnier de Graaf

Dutch physician Regnier de Graaf (1641–1673) researched the reproductive systems and identified the ovaries. He described the tiny bubbles on ovaries' surface that appear each month. Later, scientists realized that each bubble is a ripe follicle with the much smaller egg inside it.

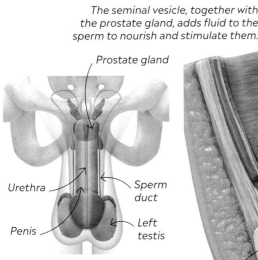

The seminal vesicle, together with the prostate gland, adds fluid to the sperm to nourish and stimulate them.

Prostate gland

Urethra

Penis

Sperm duct

Left testis

Front view of the male reproductive system

Penis and testicles

This side view shows one of two testes that hang outside the body in a skin bag called the scrotum. Inside each testis, a hormone stimulates sperm production throughout adult life. During sex, muscle contractions push sperm along two sperm ducts into the urethra and out of the penis.

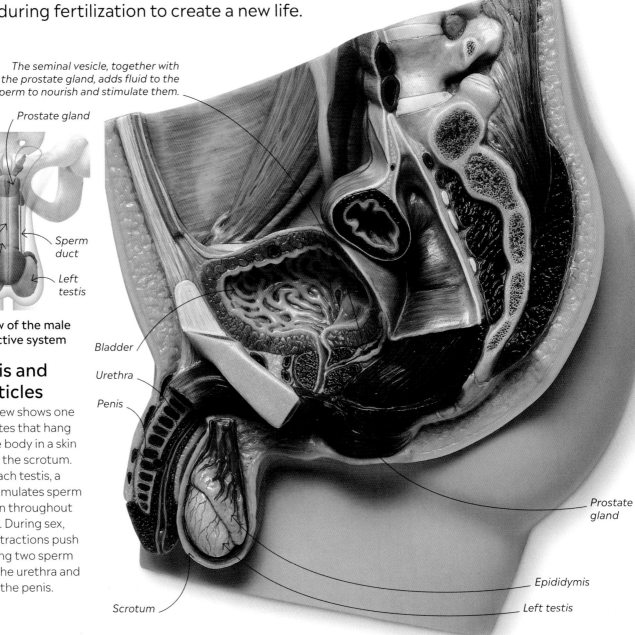

Bladder

Urethra

Penis

Prostate gland

Epididymis

Left testis

Scrotum

THE MENSTRUAL CYCLE

Every 28 days, in a menstrual (monthly) cycle, or period, an egg is released from an ovary, and the lining of the uterus thickens in order to receive the egg if it is fertilized by a sperm. The cycle is controlled by hormones released by the pituitary gland and by ovaries.

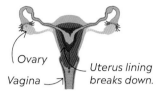

Ovary
Vagina
Uterus lining breaks down.

1 First week
The uterus lining, which thickened in the previous period, breaks down and is lost as blood flow through the vagina.

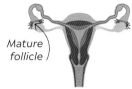

Mature follicle

2 Second week
An egg-containing follicle near the ovary's surface swells as it ripens. The uterus lining begins to grow and thicken again.

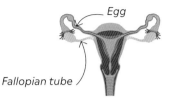

Egg
Fallopian tube

3 Third week
Ovulation occurs when the mature follicle releases its egg. The egg is moved along the fallopian tube toward the uterus.

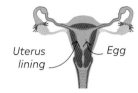

Egg
Uterus lining

4 Fourth week
The uterus lining is thick and blood-rich. If the egg is fertilized, it embeds into the lining. If not, it is broken down, and the cycle begins again.

The body's **largest cell** is the human **egg (ovum).**

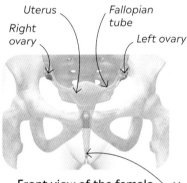

Right ovary *Uterus* *Fallopian tube* *Left ovary*

Front view of the female reproductive system

Ovaries and uterus

Ovaries release a single mature egg each month during the fertile years. It is wafted by fimbriae into the fallopian tube that leads to the uterus. If the egg meets a sperm soon after its release, the two fuse, and fertilization occurs. This results in a baby that grows inside the greatly expanding uterus (womb) and is eventually born through the vagina.

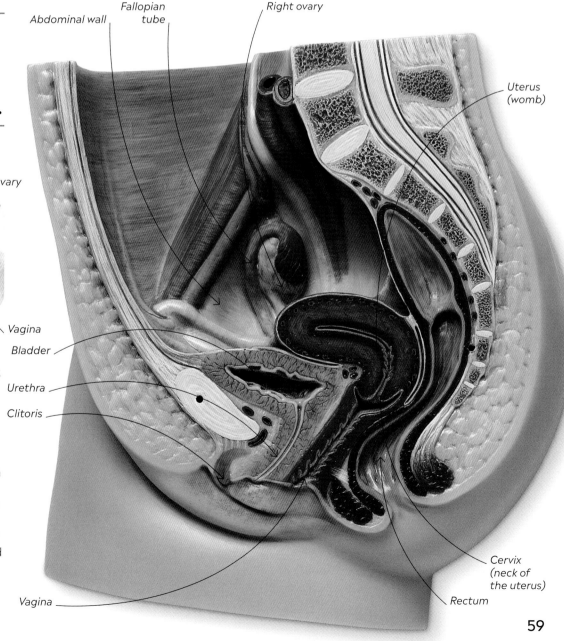

Abdominal wall *Fallopian tube* *Right ovary* *Uterus (womb)*
Vagina
Bladder
Urethra
Clitoris
Cervix (neck of the uterus)
Rectum
Vagina

A new life

Fertilization merges the DNA (genetic instructions) carried by a sperm and an egg. If the fertilized egg, no bigger than the period at the end of this sentence, settles in the lining of the uterus, it grows into an embryo and then a fetus. Around 38 weeks after fertilization, the fetus is ready to be born. Muscular contractions in the uterus push the baby out through the vagina, and the newborn baby takes its first breath.

Sperm

Egg's clear outer layer

Egg

Nucleus of the egg

As a sperm penetrates the egg, its tail drops off.

Egg fertilization

In this cutaway model, one of the sperm trying to get through the outer covering of the egg has succeeded. Its tail has dropped off, and its head (nucleus) will fuse with, or fertilize, the egg's nucleus. No other sperm can now get through.

Cluster of 16 cells

Embryo development

The fertilized egg divides into two cells, then four, eight, and so on. A week after fertilization, it implants in the uterus lining, becoming an embryo. As its cells divide, they form muscle, nerve, and other tissues. By five weeks, the embryo is the size of a pea.

A fetus growing inside the uterus **is covered in fine hair** called lanugo.

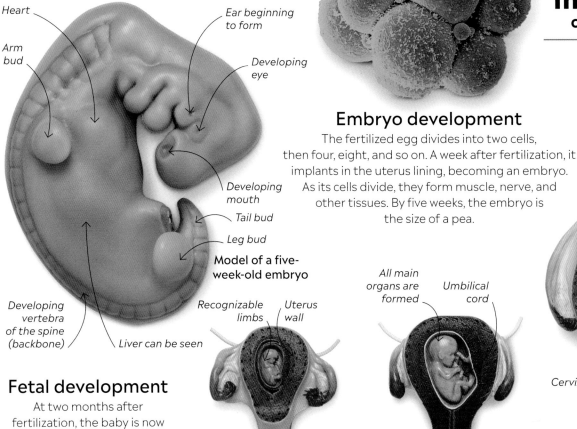

Heart

Arm bud

Ear beginning to form

Developing eye

Developing mouth

Tail bud

Leg bud

Developing vertebra of the spine (backbone)

Liver can be seen

Model of a five-week-old embryo

Fetal development

At two months after fertilization, the baby is now called a fetus. It is no bigger than a strawberry, but its major organs have formed, and its heart is beating. By around nine months, the fetus weighs about 6.5–9 lb (3–4 kg).

Recognizable limbs

Uterus wall

1 Two months
The 1-in- (2.5-cm-) long fetus has limbs, and its brain is expanding rapidly.

All main organs are formed

Umbilical cord

2 Three months
About 3 in (8 cm) long, the fetus looks human and has eyes.

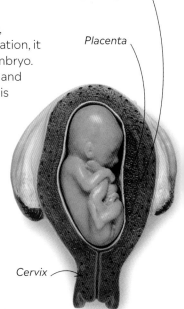

Uterus enlarges to accommodate the growing fetus

Placenta

Cervix

3 Five months
The fetus is 8 in (20 cm) long and responds to sounds by kicking and turning somersaults.

The placenta

Inside the placenta, blood vessels from the uterus and fetus pass close to each other. This allows oxygen and food to pass into the blood of the fetus through the umbilical cord. Waste from the fetus flows the other way. After the baby is born, the umbilical cord is clamped and cut. The placenta detaches and comes out.

Seeing the fetus

Ultrasound scans carried out after about 11 weeks check that all is well with the fetus developing inside the uterus. The scanner beams high-pitched but harmless sound waves into the body and detects their echoes.

Fetal blood vessels

Parental blood vessel

Placenta forms a link between the baby's blood and its parent's blood.

Umbilical arteries

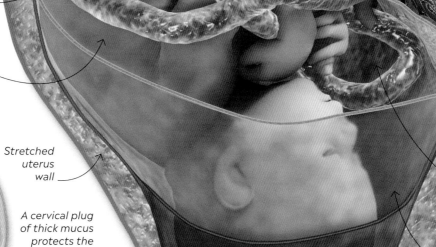

Blood vessels inside the umbilical cord carry blood to and from the fetus.

Expanded uterus presses on the parental's abdominal organs.

The fetus has grown visibly in the past two months.

Stretched uterus wall

A cervical plug of thick mucus protects the fetus from infection.

Vagina (birth canal)

Cervix will widen for the birth.

Amniotic fluid cushions the fetus.

Amnion is the membrane containing amniotic fluid in which the baby floats.

Cervix tightly shut

Fetus has turned upside down into the birth position

4 Seven months

Now about 19 in (48 cm) long, the fetus has finger- and toenails, and its eyes are open.

5 Nine months

The fetus is fully grown, at about 14 in (36 cm) long. With fully formed lungs, it is ready to be born.

Breastfeeding

Many babies are breastfed. Breast milk gives the baby the nutrients for growth and development in the months before it can eat solid food.

Growth and development

From birth to old age, we follow the same pattern of growth and body development. Physical and mental changes turn us from children into adults, and growth stops by our early 20s. The body then matures and in later years begins to deteriorate. This pattern is controlled by 23 pairs of chromosomes in the nucleus of every body cell. Each chromosome is made up of deoxyribonucleic acid (DNA). Sections of DNA, called genes, contain the coded instructions that build and maintain the body.

 **EYEWITNESS**

Rosalind Franklin
English chemist Rosalind Franklin (1920–1958) used a technique called X-ray crystallography to produce a clear image of DNA in 1952 and realized that it probably had a double-helix structure. This discovery helped US biologist James Watson and British physicist Francis Crick build the model of DNA.

Cell division

Bodies grow by making new cells. Cells reproduce by dividing in two. For most cells, this involves mitosis. Each chromosome duplicates inside a parent cell to produce an identical copy. The copies move apart, and the cell divides to produce two identical daughter cells.

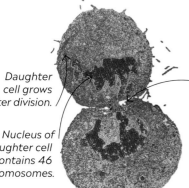

Daughter cell grows after division.

Cell's cytoplasm splits to separate daughter cells.

Nucleus of daughter cell contains 46 chromosomes.

Position of the gene that, if defective, causes cystic fibrosis

Human genome

Every human cell contains 23 chromosomes, called the genome. Each has a partner. One of each pair is from both parents. Each chromosome has the same genes as its partner, but not always identical versions. While 22 of the chromosome pairs match, the 23rd pair matches only in females and determines a person's sex.

Sex chromosome Y is passed on by the father

Most people have either XY or XX chromosomes. People with an XY pairing are usually called male, while ones with an XX pairing are usually called female.

Sex chromosome X is passed on by each parent

3 2 1 Y X 22
4 21
5 20
6 19
Map of a human genome
7 18
8 17
9 16
10 15
11 12 13 14

Chromosome 12 carries over 1,400 genes.

The banding pattern on every chromosome is produced by chemicals and used in mapping.

Genes and inheritance

If two people reproduce, they each pass on a set of genes to their child. The genes that this girl inherited from her parents are mostly identical, but some are different, so her combination of genes is unique.

Growth and the skeleton

Before birth, the skeleton is made up of either flexible cartilage or, in the skull, membranes reinforced with fibers. As the fetus grows, most of these tissues are ossified—replaced by hard bone. But the bones of the cranium (skull) are incomplete at birth and are connected by fontanels or membranes that allow the brain to grow. By early childhood, these are also ossified, and the skull bones are knitted together.

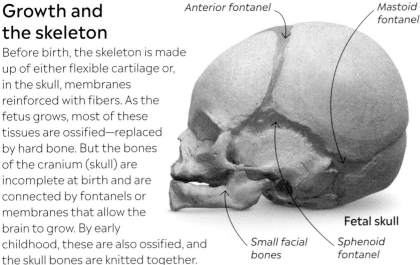

Anterior fontanel

Mastoid fontanel

Small facial bones

Sphenoid fontanel

Fetal skull

Puberty and adolescence

As children become teenagers, they experience a range of physical changes. Hormones trigger growth spurts, and the reproductive systems start functioning. Puberty forms part of adolescence, the process that also involves mental changes as teenagers turn into adults.

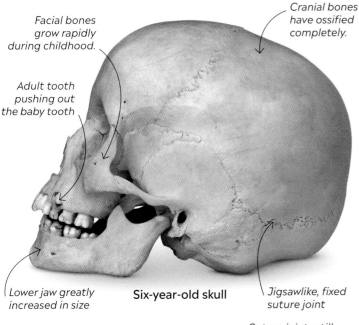

Facial bones grow rapidly during childhood.

Adult tooth pushing out the baby tooth

Cranial bones have ossified completely.

Lower jaw greatly increased in size

Six-year-old skull

Jigsawlike, fixed suture joint

Later years

As we grow older, the skin loses its springiness and develops lines and wrinkles. The heart and lungs become less efficient, joints stiffen and bones become more fragile, vision is less effective, and brain function decreases. But looking after the body with healthy food and exercise can slow these changes and help us stay healthy.

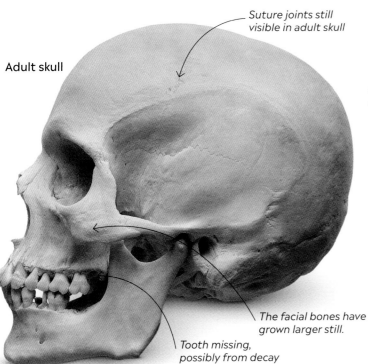

Suture joints still visible in adult skull

Adult skull

The facial bones have grown larger still.

Tooth missing, possibly from decay

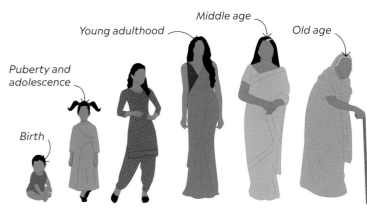

Young adulthood

Middle age

Old age

Puberty and adolescence

Birth

Life stages

Following birth and childhood, early adulthood is a time when humans are physically strongest. In middle age, the first signs of aging appear, and later in old age, the body begins to decline until, eventually, we die. With better food, health care, and sanitation in the developed world, average life expectancy is almost 80 years.

Future bodies

Advances in biology, medicine, and technology make it possible to repair or improve the human body in new ways, such as bionic limbs and artificial organs. Some changes may not be acceptable to everyone, but many predict a human future of genetic modifications, nanobots, cyborgs, and brain microchips.

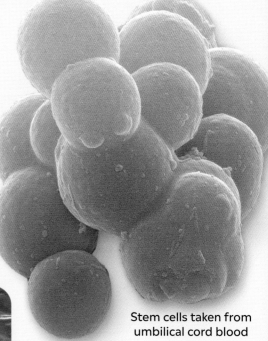

Stem cells taken from umbilical cord blood

Stem cells

Doctors believe unspecialized cells, called stem cells, can be used to repair diseased or damaged tissues in patients. Stem cells divide to produce a range of cell types and so can build many types of body tissue.

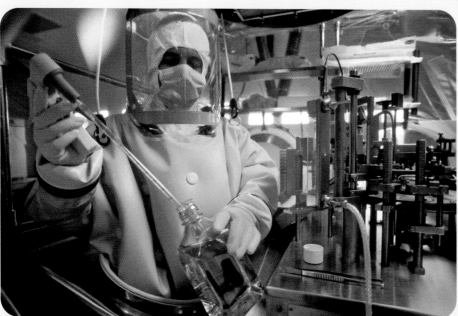

Gene editing

Each body cell contains more than 20,000 genes, the DNA instructions that build and run it. A faulty gene can cause disease. Scientists are developing ways to "edit" a gene—modifying, adding, or deleting pieces of genetic material to correct the faulty gene.

Designer children

Although controversial, it is possible to treat a sick child with a faulty gene by using stem cells from a specially designed sibling. First, a number of embryos are created through IVF (in vitro fertilization), where an egg is fertilized in a laboratory. If it does not have the faulty gene, it is placed in the mother's uterus to develop into a baby. When the child is born, stem cells in its umbilical cord are used to treat its sick sibling.

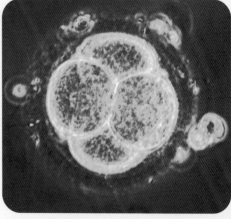

Reprogramming cells

Human embryos are a controversial source of stem cells. As an alternative, scientists have taken normal adult cells, such as blood or skin cells, and have reprogrammed them to become stem cells. It is hoped this will be a new source of stem cells to research cures for diseases.

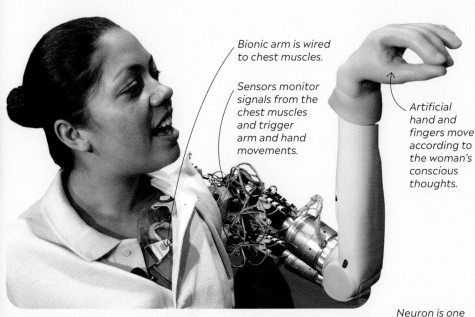

Bionic arm is wired to chest muscles.

Sensors monitor signals from the chest muscles and trigger arm and hand movements.

Artificial hand and fingers move according to the woman's conscious thoughts.

Growing organs
Currently, diseased organs are replaced by transplanting a donor organ from someone else. Using cells from the patient instead, bladder tissue was grown around a mold (above), and the new bladder was successfully implanted into the patient.

Bionic limbs
After this patient lost her arm, a bionic arm was wired to her chest muscles. When she thinks about moving her hand, messages travel to the muscles, which send out electrical signals. Sensors pass these to a tiny computer that tells her arm how to move.

Pillar supports the neuron on the microchip.

Neuron is one of a network forming a circuit with a microchip.

Brain microchips
This microchip forms an electronic circuit with neurons and can stimulate them to send and receive signals to one another and to the microchip. Future scientists might use neuron–microchip circuits to repair brain damage or boost memory or intelligence.

Cyborgs
Advances in technology have made cyborgs—human beings who are part-machine—possible. In 2004, British-Irish artist Neil Harbisson (below) became the first "legally recognized cyborg" in the world after he had an antenna implanted into his skull that let him perceive color.

Medical nanobots
Nanotechnology manipulates atoms and molecules to build tiny machines. These nanobots are self-propelled, respond to their surroundings, and can carry out tasks on their own initiative. One day, it may be possible for medical nanobots to detect, diagnose, and repair damage to the body's cells.

Eternal life?
Medical advances, such as organ replacement, together with lifestyle changes, could enable everyone to live longer. But what quality of life would there be for a 150-year-old? And how would our crowded planet support so many extra human beings?

Timeline

With each new discovery, scientists have built up a clearer picture of the body and its systems. Even so, there remain many mysteries about the workings of the human body.

Statue of Imhotep
c. 2650 BCE

c. 300,000 MILLION YEARS AGO
Modern humans first appear.

c. 2650 BCE
Ancient Egyptian Imhotep is the earliest known physician.

c. 1500 BCE
The earliest known medical text, the *Ebers Papyrus*, is written in Egypt.

c. 6th century BCE
Indian physician and surgeon Susruta writes the *Susruta Samhita*, one of the main texts of Ayurveda.

c. 420 BCE
Greek physician Hippocrates explains the importance of diagnosis.

c. 280 BCE
Herophilus of Alexandria describes the cerebrum and cerebellum of brain.

c. 200 CE
Greek-born Roman doctor Claudius Galen describes, incorrectly, how the human body works.

c. 1025
Persian doctor Ibn Sina publishes the *Al-Qanun fi al-Tibb* (*The Canon of Medicine*).

c. 1280
Syrian doctor Ibn an-Nafis shows that blood circulates around the body.

c. 1316
Italian anatomist Mondino dei Liuzzi writes his dissection guide *Anatomy*.

c. 1500
Italian artist and scientist Leonardo da Vinci makes anatomical drawings based on his own dissections.

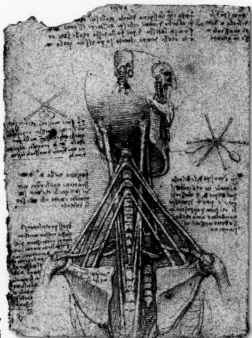

Anatomical drawing by Leonardo da Vinci

1543
Flemish doctor Andreas Vesalius publishes *On the Structure of the Human Body*, which accurately describes human anatomy.

1562
Italian anatomist Bartolomeo Eustachio describes the ear in *The Examination of the Organ of Hearing*.

c. 1590
Dutch spectacle maker Zacharias Janssen invents the microscope.

1603
Hieronymus Fabricius, an Italian anatomist, describes the structure of a vein in his book, *On the Valves of Veins*.

1628
English doctor William Harvey describes blood circulation in *On the Movement of the Heart and Blood in Animals*.

1661
Italian biologist Marcello Malpighi discovers capillaries, the small blood vessels that link arteries and veins.

1662
French philosopher René Descartes's book, *Treatise of Man*, describes the human body as a machine.

1664
English doctor Thomas Willis describes the blood supply to the brain.

1665
English physicist Robert Hooke coins the term *cell* for the smallest units of life he sees through his microscope.

1672
Dutch anatomist Regnier de Graaf describes the female reproductive system.

1674–1677
Antoni van Leeuwenhoek, a Dutch microscopist, describes human blood cells and sperm cells.

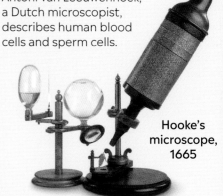

Hooke's microscope, 1665

1691
English doctor Clopton Havers describes the microscopic structure of bones.

1800
French doctor Marie-François Bichat shows that organs are made of groups of cells called tissues.

1811
Scottish anatomist Charles Bell shows that nerves are bundles of nerve cells.

1816
French doctor René Laënnec invents the stethoscope.

1833
U.S. army surgeon William Beaumont publishes the results of his experiments into the mechanism of digestion.

1837
Czech biologist Johannes Purkinje observes neurons in the brain's cerebellum.

1842
British surgeon William Bowman describes the microscopic structure and workings of the kidney.

1848
French scientist Claude Bernard describes the workings of the liver.

1851
German physicist Hermann von Helmholtz invents the ophthalmoscope, an instrument for looking inside the eye.

1861
French doctor Paul Pierre Broca identifies the area of the brain that controls speech.

An early ophthalmoscope

1878
German scientist Wilhelm Kühne coins the term *enzyme* for substances that speed up chemical reactions inside living things.

1895
German physicist Wilhelm Roentgen discovers X-rays.

1901
Karl Landsteiner, an Austrian-American doctor, identifies blood groups, paving the way for more successful blood transfusions.

1905
British scientist Ernest Starling coins the term *hormone*.

1926
U.S. physiologist Walter Cannon coins the term *homeostasis* for mechanisms that maintain a stable state inside the body.

1933
German electrical engineer Ernst Ruska invents the electron microscope.

1952
In the U.S., Paul Zoll invents the pacemaker to control an irregular heartbeat.

1953
U.S. biologist James Watson and British physicist Francis Crick discover the double-helix structure of DNA.

1954
U.S. surgeon Joseph E. Murray performs the first kidney transplant, on identical twins.

A wounded U.S. soldier receives a blood transfusion during World War II.

1958
British doctor Ian Donald uses ultrasound scanning to check the health of a fetus.

1961
U.S. scientist Marshall Nirenberg cracks the genetic code of DNA.

1967
Magnetic resonance imaging (MRI) is first used to see soft tissues inside the body.

1971
Computed tomography (CT) scanning first produces images of the human brain.

1980
Doctors perform "keyhole" surgery inside the body through small incisions with the assistance of an endoscope.

1980s
Positron emission tomography (PET) scans first produce images of brain activity.

1982
The first artificial heart, invented by U.S. scientist Robert Jarvik, is transplanted into a patient.

1984
French scientist Luc Montagnier discovers the human immunodeficiency virus (HIV) that results in AIDS.

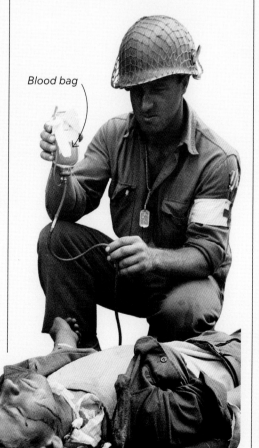

Blood bag

2001
Scientists perform the first germline gene transfer in animals, to prevent faulty genes from being passed on to offspring.

2002
Gene therapy is used to treat an inherited immunodeficiency disease that leaves the body unable to fight against infection.

Computer display of DNA sequencing

2003
Scientists publish results of the Human Genome Project, identifying the DNA sequence of a full set of chromosomes.

2006
A urinary bladder, grown in the laboratory from a patient's own cells, is successfully transplanted to replace a damaged organ.

2007
Thought to be useless, the appendix is shown to hold a back-up reservoir of bacteria that is essential to the workings of the large intestine.

2008
Dutch geneticist Marjolein Kreik becomes the first woman to have her genome sequenced.

2010
DaVinci, a surgical robot, performs the world's first all-robotic surgery in Montreal, Canada.

2013
Scientists in Japan create a functional human liver from skin and blood stem cells.

2019
Scientists at Tel Aviv University in Israel print the first human heart using a patient's own cells.

2021
An mRNA vaccine (Pfizer COVID-19 vaccine) is used widely for the first time.

Find out more

Listen for news stories about the latest discoveries in medical science and documentaries about the human body and how it works. Look out for special exhibitions at museums near you or search in your local library and online. You also have your own body to study! Take good care of it by eating healthily and exercising regularly.

The old operating theater

This 19th-century operating theater at the old site of St. Thomas's hospital in London predates anesthetics. Surgeons worked quickly to minimize a patient's suffering during amputations and other operations. Medical students watched from tiered stands around the operating table.

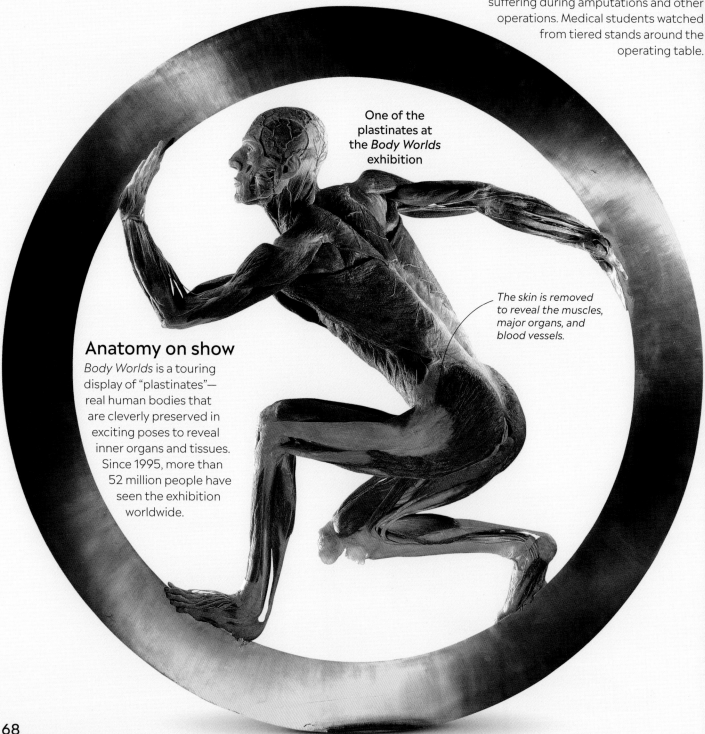

One of the plastinates at the *Body Worlds* exhibition

The skin is removed to reveal the muscles, major organs, and blood vessels.

Anatomy on show

Body Worlds is a touring display of "plastinates"—real human bodies that are cleverly preserved in exciting poses to reveal inner organs and tissues. Since 1995, more than 52 million people have seen the exhibition worldwide.

Walk-in body

At the Health Museum in Houston, Texas, visitors can take a larger-than-life tour through the human body—including this arch created by a giant backbone and ribs. The Amazing Body Pavilion features exciting interactive experiences, including a giant eyeball and a walk-through brain, and hands-on exhibits about health and well-being.

Giant body sculpture

Australian artist Ron Mueck's *Mask II* is a giant self-portrait of the artist sleeping and is sculpted from resin and fiberglass. Visits to art galleries to see sculptures and paintings can reveal much about the variety of the human form.

An acrobat's brain controls balance, posture, and precise movements.

Muscle and joint flexibility is achieved by constant training.

Acrobatics

Watching ballet and circus shows like the *Cirque du Soleil* provides a great opportunity to marvel at the strength, flexibility, and grace of the human body.

PLACES TO VISIT

CITÉ DES SCIENCES, PARIS, FRANCE
- Interactive displays of the human body
- Detailed explorations of DNA discoveries

FRANKLIN INSTITUTE, PHILADELPHIA, PENNSYLVANIA
- Giant walk-through heart
- Melting humans exhibit showing internal organs and systems

HALL OF SCIENCE, NEW YORK, NEW YORK
- Infrared camera maps your body's hot spots
- Lots of hands-on exhibits to explore perceptions, molecules, and health

THE HUNTERIAN, GLASGOW, UK
- Life-size plaster casts of dissections
- Anatomical specimens preserved in jars
- Scientific instruments

SCIENCE MUSEUM, LONDON, UK
- *Who Am I?* gallery on genetics and identity
- Exhibits on the history of medicine

DUNDEE SCIENCE CENTER, DUNDEE, UK
- Interactive keyhole surgery exhibit
- Face-morphing

MANIPAL MUSEUM OF ANATOMY AND PATHOLOGY, INDIA
- Preserved human specimens
- Anatomical models and charts

LA SPECOLA, FLORENCE, ITALY
- Anatomical wax models of dissected bodies

Early stethoscope at the Science Museum, London

USEFUL WEBSITES

- A fun, animated guide to the human body:
  www.brainpop.com/health
- A comprehensive guide to blood, from platelets to plasma—this website has several other body topics too:
  health.howstuffworks.com/blood
- A website for young people, with tips on keeping healthy:
  kidshealth.org/kids

Glossary

ABDOMEN The lower part of the torso between the chest and hips.

ADOLESCENCE The period of physical and mental changes that occur during the teenage years and mark the transition from childhood to adulthood.

ALVEOLI The microscopic air bags in the lungs through which oxygen enters the blood and carbon dioxide leaves it.

AMNIOTIC FLUID A liquid that surrounds the fetus inside the uterus. It protects the fetus from knocks and jolts.

ANATOMY The study of the structure of the human body.

ANTIBODY A substance released by cells called lymphocytes that marks an invading pathogen or germ for destruction.

ARTERY A blood vessel that carries blood from the heart toward the body tissues.

ATOM The smallest particle of an element, such as carbon or hydrogen, that can exist.

BACTERIA A type of microorganism. Some bacteria are pathogens (germs) that cause disease in humans.

BILE A fluid delivered from the liver to the intestine to aid digestion.

BLOOD VESSEL A tube, such as an artery, vein, or capillary, that transports blood around the body.

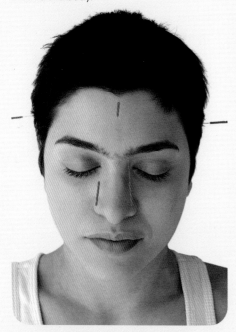

Acupuncture needles inserted into the skin to provide pain relief

CAPILLARY A microscopic blood vessel that links arteries to veins.

CARTILAGE A tough, flexible tissue that supports the nose, ears, and other body parts and covers bones' ends in joints.

CELL One of the trillions of microscopic living units that make up a human body.

CHROMOSOME One of 46 packages of DNA found inside most body cells.

CHYME A souplike liquid that is formed of part-digested food in the stomach and released into the small intestine.

DIAPHRAGM The dome-shaped muscle between the thorax and the abdomen.

DIGESTION The breakdown of the complex molecules in food into simple nutrients, such as sugars, which are absorbed into the bloodstream and used by cells.

DISSECTION The careful cutting open of a dead body to study its internal structure.

DNA (DEOXYRIBONUCLEIC ACID) A molecule containing genes (instructions) for building and running the body's cells.

EMBRYO An unborn baby during the first eight weeks of development after fertilization.

ENDOCRINE GLAND A collection of cells, such as the thyroid gland, that release hormones into the bloodstream.

Model of an enzyme involved in digesting food

ENZYME A protein that acts as a biological catalyst to speed up the rate of chemical reactions inside and outside cells.

FECES The semisolid waste made up of undigested food, dead cells, and bacteria removed from the body through the anus.

FERTILIZATION The fusion of a sperm and an egg to make a new human being.

Blood vessels supplying the lower arm and hand

FETUS A baby growing inside the uterus from its ninth week until its birth.

FOLLICLE A group of cells inside an ovary that surrounds and nurtures an egg. Also, a pit in the skin from which a hair grows.

GAS EXCHANGE The movement of oxygen from the lungs into the bloodstream and of carbon dioxide from the bloodstream into the lungs.

GENE One of 20,000–25,000 instructions contained within a cell's chromosomes that control its construction and operation.

GLAND A group of cells that create chemical substances, such as hormones or sweat, and release them into the body.

GLUCOSE A type of sugar that circulates in the blood and provides cells with their major source of energy.

HOMEOSTASIS The maintenance of stable conditions, such as temperature or amount of water or glucose, inside the body so that cells can work normally.

HORMONE A chemical messenger that is made by an endocrine gland and carried in the blood to its target tissue or organ.

IMMUNE SYSTEM A collection of cells in the circulatory and lymphatic systems that track and destroy pathogens (germs).

KERATIN The tough, waterproof protein in cells that make up the hair, nails, and upper epidermis of the skin.

LYMPH The fluid that flows through the lymphatic system from tissues to the blood.

MEMBRANE A thin layer of tissue that covers or lines an external or internal body surface. Also, a cell's outer layer.

MENINGES The protective membranes that cover the brain and spinal cord.

MENSTRUAL CYCLE The sequence of body changes, repeated roughly every 28 days, that prepare a reproductive system to receive a fertilized egg.

METABOLISM The chemical processes that take place in every cell in the body, resulting, for example, in growth and the release of energy.

MOLECULE A tiny particle that is made up of two or more linked atoms.

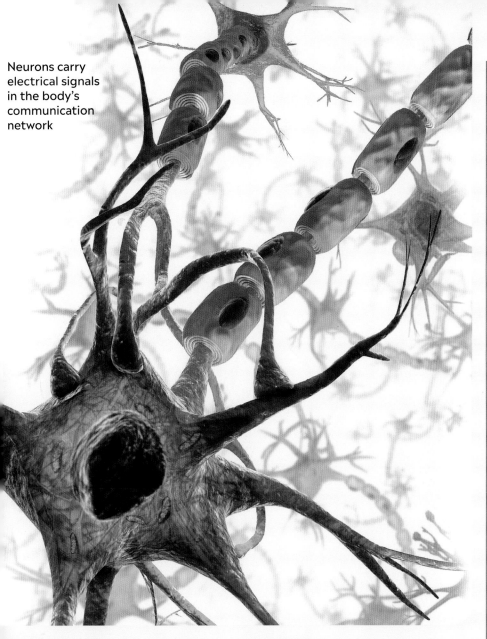

Neurons carry electrical signals in the body's communication network

SURGERY The treatment of disease or injury by direct intervention, often using surgical instruments to open the body.

SUTURE An immovable joint, such as that between two skull bones.

SYNAPSE A junction between two neurons, where a nerve signal is passed from cell to cell. The neurons are very close at a synapse, but they do not touch.

SYSTEM A collection of linked organs that work together to carry out a specific task or tasks. An example is the digestive system.

TISSUE An organized group of one type of cell, or similar types of cells, that works together to perform a particular function.

TORSO The central part of the body, also known as the trunk, made up of the thorax and abdomen.

UMBILICAL CORD The ropelike structure that connects a fetus to the placenta.

URINE A liquid produced by the kidneys that contains wastes, surplus water, and salts removed from the blood.

VEIN A blood vessel that carries blood from the body tissues toward the heart.

VIRUS A nonliving pathogen that causes diseases, such as colds and measles, in humans.

X-RAY A form of radiation that reveals bones when projected through the body onto film.

NEURON One of the billions of nerve cells that make up the nervous system.

NUTRIENT A substance, such as glucose (sugar), needed in the diet to maintain normal body functioning and good health.

OLFACTORY To do with the sense of smell.

ORGAN A body part, such as the heart, that is made up of two or more types of tissue and carries out a particular function.

OSSIFICATION The formation of bone, replacing cartilage with bone tissue.

PATHOGEN A germ, a type of microorganism, such as a bacterium or virus, that causes disease in humans.

PHYSICIAN A doctor.

PHYSIOLOGY The study of the body's functions and processes—how it works.

PLACENTA The organ that delivers food and oxygen to a fetus from its parent. Half develops from the parent's body, and half is part of the fetus's body.

PREGNANCY The period of time between an embryo implanting in the uterus and a baby being born, usually 38–40 weeks.

PUBERTY The part of adolescence when a child's body changes into an adult's and the reproductive system starts to work.

SPERM One type of sex cells, also called spermatozoa.

SPINAL CORD A column of nervous tissue inside the spine. It relays nerve signals between the brain and body.

Sutures, or jigsaw-like joints in the skull

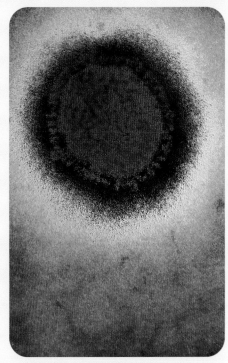

TEM of an influenza (flu) virus magnified 135,000 times

Index

Acknowledgments

Dorling Kindersley would like to thank the following people for their help with making the book:
Camilla Hallinan, Upamanyu Das, and Deeksha Micek for editorial assistance; Aparajita Sen for design assistance; Rajeev Doshi at Medimation (pp.26-27, 40-41, and 50-51) and Arran Lewis (pp.38-39) for illustrations; DK Diversity, Equity, & Inclusion team for authenticity checks; Hazel Beynon for proofreading; and Elizabeth Wise for the index.

The publisher would like to thank the following for their kind permission to reproduce their photographs:
(Key: a-above; b-below/bottom; c-center; f-far; l-left; r-right; t-top)

akg-images: 9cl, 11tl; **Alamy Images:** Art Directors & TRIP 44bc; Chronicle 32bc; Mauritius images GmbH / Rene Mattes 8tl; Mary Evans Picture Library 9tl, 10cl, 12tr, 18cla, 30br, 33ca, 34bc, 46cb, 56tr; Dennis Hallinan 66bc; The London Art Archive 55tr; PHOTOTAKE Inc. 7c, 26bl, 29cra, 60c; The Print Collector 12c, 16tl, 50tr; Science History Images 42br; **The Art Archive:** Bodleian Library, Oxford / Ashmole 399 folio 34r, 10tl; **BIU Santé Médecine:** 11crb; **The Bridgeman Art Library:** Bibliothèque de la Faculté de Médecine, Paris / Archives Charmet 46c; Bibliothèque Nationale, Paris 8cr; **Corbis:** Bettmann 24cl, 41c, 50cl, 67bc; Christophe Boisvieux 31cra; EPA / Geoff Caddick 69bl; Frank Lane Picture Agency / Ron Boardman 13crb; The Gallery Collection 44crb; Hulton-Deutsch Collection 22tr, 26cl; Reuters / David Gray 69c; Ariel Skelley 62bl; Visuals Unlimited 7cr, 18clb, 19tr; Zefa / Flynn Larsen 33br; **DK Images:** The British Museum, London 42tl; The British Museum, London / Peter Hayman 8-9b, 46cl; Combustion 46-47c, 71tl; Courtesy of Denoyer - Geppert Intl. / Geoff Brightling 55bc; Donks Models / Geoff Dann 13crt; Arran Lewis 38-39; Medi-Mation 40-41c, 50-51bc; Courtesy of the Museum of Natural History of the University of Florence, Zoology section 'La Specola' /

Liberto Perugi 37c, 44tr; Old Operating Theatre Museum, London / Steve Gorton 2cb, 4tr, 10-11b, 11cl; Courtesy of The Science Museum, London/ Adrian Whicher 8cl; Courtesy of The Science Museum, London / Dave King 3tl, 12cl, 12cr, 66cr, 69cr; Courtesy of The Science Museum, London / John Lepine 67tl; Dreamstime.com Okea 4cr, 53c; **Depositphotos Inc:** Ypsg2008 9tr; **Dreamstime.com:** Galina Barskaya 63c; Fizkes 63tr; Witoon Buttre 6tl; Albund (r/Background) 24; Yevgeniy Repiashenko (r/Girl) 24; Mamahoohooba 35tr; **Getty Images:** AFP / Andre Durand 14bc; AFP / Damien Meyer 21br; Ander Gillenea / AFP 17tr; ER Productions Limited / DigitalVision 15tl; Henry Guttmann 11tr; The Image Bank / Johannes Kroemer 70bl; Nick Laham 53tr; Win McNamee 65tl; Michael Ochs Archives 48cb; Popperfoto 28clb; Rosdiana Ciaravolo / Getty Images Entertainment 65bl; Science Faction / David Scharf 33cr; Science Faction / Rawlins - CMSP 64crb; Stone / Ron Boardman 13bl; Taxi / Emmanuel Faure 15cbl; Skynesher / E+ 42bl; Time Life Pictures / Mansell 37br; Topical Press Agency 41cr; Universal History Archive 62cra; Visuals Unlimited / Michael Gabridge 71bl; **Getty Images / iStock:** Deepak Sethi / E+ 20tl; **Gunther von Hagens' BODY WORLDS, Institute for Plastination, Heidelberg, Germany, www.bodyworlds. com:** 68b; **Courtesy of The Health Museum, Houston:** 69tl; **iStockphoto.com:** Roberto A. Sanchez 16bl; Jaroslaw Wojcik 64bc; **Johns Hopkins University:** Muyinatu Lediju Bell bc; **Minoru Shirota:** Minoru Shirota from Korinshoin Shokuhin Kogyo, Vol. 10, No. 17 (1967) / Public Domain 55tr; **Courtesy of The Old Operating Theatre, Museum & Herb Garret, London:** 68tl; **PA Photos:** AP Photo / Brian Walker 65tr; **Photolibrary:** Imagestate / David South 65bc; **Photo Scala, Florence:** The Museum of Modern Art, New York 30cra; **Science Photo Library:** 23c, 36tr, 58tr; Juergen Berger 64tr; Biology Media 25cr; Scott Camazine, Sue Trainor 18tl; Chemical Design 47c; CNRI 39tr, 41bc, 49cbl, 49fcl; Christian Darkin 65crb; Equinox Graphics 70cb; Eye of Science 55tl;

Simon Fraser 15r; GCa 17br; Steve Gschmeissner 19br, 32tr, 51tl; Innerspace Imaging 50bl; ISM / Alain Pol 57cr; Christian Jegou Publiphoto Diffusion 6tl; Nancy Kedersha 30-31t; James King-Holmes 67cr; Patrick Landmann 64cl; RIJKSMuseum 12bc; Dr. Najeeb Layyous 61tl; Astrid & Hanns-Frieder Michler 41cl; Prof. P. Motta / Dept. of Anatomy / University 'La Sapienza', Rome 37t, 39br, 54cl; MPI Biochemistry/ Volker Steger 65c; Dr Gopal Murti 62clb; NIBSC 71br; Omikron 35bl; US National Library of Medicine 28tr; Wellcome Department of Cognitive Neurology 15cl; Zephyr 14tr; **Shutterstock.com:** Dragon Images 13cb; **Still Pictures:** The Medical File / Charles Brooks 14cl; Ed Reschkè 21cb; **Wellcome Library, London:** 6bl, 16cla, 22tl, 23bc, 23tc, 36c.

© 2008, by SOMSO models, www.somso.com: 2tr, 3tr, 4cla, 4cra, 18cr, 19ca, 24c, 27br, 30bl, 31bcr, 32br, 46cl, 53bc, 53bl, 56bl, 56br, 58br, 59br, 60b, 61bl.

All other images © Dorling Kindersley

For further information, see:
www.dkimages.com

SOMSO
MODELLE
SINCE 1876